CAREERS IN

HOMELAND SECURITY

CAREERS IN

HOMELAND SECURITY

BY ADAM WOOG

Cavendish
Square

New York

For my daughter, Leah, who inspired it.

With special thanks to Carlos Perea, academic adviser for
the Department of Criminology and Criminal Justice at University of Maryland, College Park.

Published in 2014 by Cavendish Square Publishing, LLC
303 Park Avenue South, Suite 1247, New York, NY 10010

LIBRARY OF CONGRESS CATALOGING-IN-PUBLICATION DATA
Woog, Adam, 1953-
Careers in homeland security / Adam Woog.
p. cm. — (Law and order jobs)
Includes bibliographical references and index.
Summary: "Provides a comprehensive look at the careers available within the Department of Homeland Security"—Provided by publisher.
ISBN 978-1-62712-422-5 (hardcover) ISBN 978-1-62712-423-2 (paperback) ISBN 978-1-62712-424-9 (ebook)
1. United States. Department of Homeland Security—Vocational guidance—Juvenile literature. 2. United States. Department of Homeland Security—Officials and employees—Juvenile literature. 3. Civil defense—United States—Juvenile literature. 4. National defense—United States—Juvenile literature. I. Title. HV6432.4.W66 2014
363.34023'73—dc23 2011028732

ART DIRECTOR: Anahid Hamparian   SERIES DESIGNER: Michael Nelson
LAYOUT DESIGN: Joseph Macri   EDITOR: Dean Miller
Photo research by Marybeth Kavanaugh

The photographs in this book are used by permission and through the courtesy of:
Cover photo by David Duprey/AP Photo. Getty Images: Paul J. Richards/AFP (seal), back cover, front cover, 3; Alex Wong, 8, 12, 37; Scott Olson/Staff/Getty Images News, 51; Corbis: Charlie Neuman/ZUMA Press, 20; J. Emilio Flores, 58; Liz Hafalia/San Francisco Chronicle, 93; Landov: Gary C. Caskey/UPI, 31; Tom Sperduto/UPI, 2–3, 81; The Image Works: The Star-Ledger/Tony Kurdzuk, 40; DoD/Roger-Viollet, 68; Jocelyn Augustino©FEMA/Lightroom/Topfoto, 87; Photo Researchers, Inc.: David R. Frazier, 54; Newscom: Robert Galbraith/AFP/Getty Images, 70.

Printed in the United States of America

CONTENTS

KEEPING THE HOMELAND SAFE

ANYONE WHO HAS TRAVELED BY AIR IN OR OUT OF the United States in the last ten years or so—and that's a lot of people—will have noticed some dramatic changes. Long lines for security checks, passengers taking off their shoes, stepped-up X-ray examinations of baggage, identity checks, restrictions on the amount of liquid passengers can carry onto the plane— all these and more are sure signs of one of the twenty-first century's biggest concerns: ensuring the safety of the nation.

Those airport restrictions are just the tip of a very large iceberg. The terrorist attacks of September 11, 2001, were not just devastating for the victims' families and friends. They also had extraordinary and long-lasting repercussions both in the United States and around the world. The aftermath of the tragedy shook and profoundly changed the nation's politics, social relations, foreign policies, and governmental structure. The same is true for the nation's economy. Rich Cooper, business liaison director at the U.S. Department of Homeland Security, comments, "I'd say there's not an industry or business out there today that's not impacted by homeland security."

Some of the changes are readily apparent to the average person, notably those security checks at airports. Not all the changes have been so noticeable. For example, America has new (and controversial) laws about how far federal and local law enforcement agencies can go in the course of investigating people suspected of being threats to national security.

More specifically, the events of 9/11 have had a profound impact on the organization and purpose of the American government's security agencies. In some cases, existing agencies have shifted their priorities to new targets. For example, the role the Federal Bureau of Investigation (FBI) plays in law enforcement has changed significantly. Much of the FBI's focus is now on the detection and halting of terrorist threats from both domestic and foreign sources.

An even greater change has been the sweeping reorganization of agencies devoted to protecting America's borders and inland regions. That change began shortly after 9/11. The first step came early in 2002, when the administration of President George W. Bush enacted the Homeland Security Act. This was the bill that led directly to the formation of the huge new entity known as the U.S. Department of Homeland Security.

DHS, as it is known, was designed to bring many separate federal security agencies under a single umbrella. Some of these, such as the Coast Guard, already existed. Others, including the Transportation Security Administration, were created from scratch.

The new, consolidated department's fundamental purpose was—and still is—to focus on the prevention of terrorist attacks inside American borders, on minimizing the damage

The events of September 11, 2001, led President George W. Bush to sign the Homeland Security Act in early 2002.

if attacks do happen, and on speeding the recovery from any such attacks. The statement announcing the department's formation describes its mission:

> The mission of the Office [of Homeland Security] will be to develop and coordinate the implementation of a comprehensive national strategy to secure the United States from terrorist threats or attacks. The Office will

coordinate the executive branch's efforts to detect, prepare for, prevent, protect against, respond to, and recover from terrorist attacks within the United States.

DHS's responsibilities have since expanded to include other areas of security and safety. It now has six official functions:

- Enforcing and administering immigration laws
- Preparing for and responding to natural disasters and other crises
- Preventing terrorism and enhancing security against it
- Safeguarding and securing cyberspace
- Securing and managing national borders
- Fulfilling any other related duties

The involvement of DHS in the first declared function, fighting the war on terrorism, is largely an acknowledgment that the battle cannot be fought only abroad. (Military and intelligence operations outside the United States are the responsibilities of other entities, such as the Department of Defense and the Central Intelligence Agency.) Instead, DHS recognizes that security must also be guaranteed on and within the nation's borders. In 2010 Homeland Security Secretary Janet Napolitano commented, "The old view that 'if we fight the terrorists abroad, we won't have to fight them here' is just that—the old view."

Guarding against terrorism takes many forms for the agencies within DHS, and there are plenty of options for careers. Homeland Security's Rich Cooper gives examples: "In terms of careers, homeland security has an impact in so many ways. It's everything from an airport screener to an intelligence analyst to a person who looks at **infrastructure** and how we can ready it. It's such a broad panorama."

So, if being part of the organization devoted to homeland security appeals to you, there is also a wide range of options. For example, one of the major divisions of DHS, Immigration and Customs Enforcement (ICE), acts to protect the nation from terrorist attacks and at the same time is responsible for the investigation and enforcement of regulations concerning the smuggling into the country of people, drugs, animals, plants, and any other illegal substance or living thing that might be brought in against the country's best interest.

Another example is the Federal Emergency Management Agency (FEMA). FEMA focuses on preparing for natural disasters such as earthquakes and storms, rescuing people who have experienced such a crisis, and helping communities rebuild afterward.

Still another DHS agency having several goals that do not relate directly to the prevention of acts of terrorism is the Coast Guard. Much of its work involves search-and-rescue missions along the nation's major waterways.

The Coast Guard offers the type of work within DHS that is often dangerous, but also especially exciting and rewarding. For example, one of its most interesting and challenging jobs is that of rescue swimmer. As the title implies, rescue swimmers venture out into the open water—typically lowered from helicopters—to save people in distress.

"Aviation survival technician" is the official title for Coast Guard rescue swimmers. Before his retirement, Wil Milam was a member of this elite group. He had come to the job as a result of a personal experience.

In the 1990s Milam was a navy man stationed in southern California. One day when he was off duty, Milam and a friend took out a small boat, looking for a good spot to surf. A wave flipped them over and left the pair stranded in the water—but a Coast Guard helicopter flew in and rescued them.

The aftermath of that incident wasn't just that the Coast Guard had saved the sailors' lives. The moment had a profound effect on the rest of Milam's career. In an article in *Time* magazine, he recalled, "I'm looking at the guy sitting in the door of the helicopter and I am thinking, man, what a cool job! I want that guy's job!"

He got it.

Being a rescue swimmer is hardly the only cool job in the Department of Homeland Security, nor is it the only important one. There are plenty of others.

Janet Napolitano was appointed by President Barack Obama to head the Department of Homeland Security. In addition to securing the nation's borders, the department deals with many threats, among them public health concerns such as the H1N1 virus, or swine flu, which threatened to become an epidemic in 2009.

THE
BIG PICTURE

TWENTY-TWO MAJOR AGENCIES AND OTHER organizations—a total of 187—are under Homeland Security's umbrella. They focus on such areas as science and technology, helping new immigrants learn English and otherwise adjust to life in the United States, emergency preparedness, nuclear detection, law enforcement training, risk reduction, security of federal buildings and property, protecting goods and people entering the United States, communications, health and medicine, intelligence and analysis, and **cybersecurity**.

The sheer size of DHS makes it the nation's third largest cabinet-level department. Only the departments of Defense and Veterans Affairs are bigger. As of early 2011, DHS as a whole employed more than 230,000 people. They work at twenty-nine field offices, dozens of other facilities across the country, and the department's headquarters in Washington, D.C.

Given the number of DHS employees and the agency's vast responsibilities, such a huge entity has a huge budget, too. For the fiscal year 2011, Congress authorized a budget of $98.8 billion for the Department of Homeland Security.

COOPERATION

Not all the agencies within DHS operate as completely separate entities. There is often a high degree of overlap among them, and various agencies frequently cooperate with one another and with other government departments.

For example, Immigration and Customs Enforcement (ICE) and Customs and Border Protection (CBP) routinely work together closely. The two agencies have responsibilities that are related but separate. Notably, CBP agents monitor people and cargo coming into the country, watching for illegal weapons and enforcing immigration laws at and near borders. (ICE's mandate is to enforce these policies and laws elsewhere in the United States.) CBP also collects import duties and inspects the commercial transport of animals and plants across U.S. borders, making sure that no diseases from these sources are carried into the country.

The various DHS agencies also try to coordinate their efforts with other law enforcement organizations outside the federal government. These include their government counterparts in other countries, as well as nongovernmental organizations (**NGOs**) such as the International Red Cross and other relief agencies. The purpose of this coordination, of course, is to ensure the smooth and efficient operation of law enforcement and disaster relief. In the agency's report for one quarter of 2010, Secretary Napolitano comments

[E]very day, ensuring the security of the homeland requires the interaction of multiple Federal departments and agencies, as well as operational collaboration across Federal, State, local, tribal, and territorial governments, nongovernmental organizations, and the private sector. This collaboration and cooperation undergirds our security posture at our borders and ports, our preparedness in our communities, and our ability to effectively react to crises.

Part of this effort to coordinate DHS's activities with outside organizations has been to take on a major role in the creation of a highly sophisticated national network of law enforcement agencies. The purpose of this network is to collect and analyze intelligence on a broad spectrum of Americans, as well as citizens of other countries. This information may or may not be related to terrorist activity. The network also tracks illegal aliens trying to cross the border from Mexico.

Although CBP has its headquarters in Washington, D.C., like other agencies, most CBP agents work in remote regions where an unusual skill set is needed to find illegal immigrants who try to hide their movements. Kenneth St. Germain, a Border Patrol agent in Arizona, comments, "It's a pretty good amount of desert, sand dunes, and cacti. And because our area is sand, we chase footprints. It's tracking skills."

Altogether, some four thousand federal, state, and local organizations are part of this network. Many of these organizations, such as local police departments, have existed for a long time. They have shifted at least some of their focus toward the goal of fighting terrorism. However, roughly one-fourth of the agencies in the national network were formed after 9/11, specifically for counterterrorism purposes.

As part of this project, in 2011 DHS trained about 1,400 local law enforcement officers in techniques for analyzing information about private citizens that may be relevant to the goal of preventing terrorism. Homeland Security is also providing local agencies with a daily flow of information bulletins discussing possible terror threats. Furthermore, DHS has given out some $31 billion in grants to state and local governments to help them improve their homeland security capabilities.

The network has proved to be highly controversial. Some critics have charged that it is an invasion of the privacy of Americans who have no connections with terrorism. However, many law enforcement professionals defend the network as necessary and effective. One member of this group, Memphis Police Department director Larry Godwin, told reporters from the *Washington Post*, "We have our own terrorists, and they are taking lives every day. . . . [W]e don't have suicide bombers—not yet. But you need to remain vigilant and realize how vulnerable you can be if you let up."

To this end, DHS is constantly working to improve and upgrade its departments and procedures. For example, early in its existence the agency set up a program designed to alert Americans to potential terrorist threats. This was a color-coded set of risk levels, from red (severe risk) to green (low risk). However, the system proved to be ineffective and cumbersome. So in the spring of 2011 a simpler system was unveiled, with only two levels: "elevated" and "imminent." An "elevated" alert will warn the public of a serious potential threat against the country but won't specify targets (to prevent critical information from reaching potential enemies). Meanwhile, an "imminent" alert will be a warning of a credible, specific, and impending (or ongoing) threat.

These warnings will be sent to law enforcement officials and the public through a variety of sources, including the social media platforms Twitter and Facebook. An article in the *Los Angeles Times* quoted DHS Secretary Napolitano as saying: "When a credible threat develops that could impact the public, we will tell you and provide whatever information we can so that you know how to keep yourselves, your families and your communities safe."

THE SEAL OF DHS

The seal of the Department of Homeland Security is rich with symbols of its primary mission: to prevent attacks and protect Americans on the land, in the sea, and in the air.

Its centerpiece is a white American eagle on a circular blue field. The eagle's outstretched wings are breaking through a red ring. This symbolizes the intent that the new department, DHS, will break through traditional bureaucracy.

As on the Great Seal of the United States, the eagle's talon on the left holds an olive branch with thirteen leaves and thirteen seeds; on the right are thirteen arrows. The olive branch symbolizes a desire for peace; the arrows a willingness to defend.

On the eagle's breast is a three-sectioned shield representing sky, land, and sea. The dark blue sky has twenty-two stars to represent the twenty-two main entities of the department.

17

JOB OPPORTUNITIES

The twenty-two main agencies of DHS and each of the many subgroups are vital parts of a huge operation. Though the activities of many agencies, and the careers available there, are interesting, we'll focus on four that have high profiles: the Transportation Security Administration (TSA), Immigration and Customs Enforcement (ICE), the U.S. Coast Guard (USCG), and the Federal Emergency Management Agency (FEMA).

There is no shortage of job opportunities in the other Homeland Security agencies, either. Taken together, the DHS jobs represent diverse areas, including the following:

- Fraud detection
- Intelligence gathering and analysis
- Law enforcement and legal matters
- Medicine
- Prevention of smuggling of illegal aliens, drugs, weapons, and endangered animals

Some Homeland Security employees have what is essentially a desk job, such as forensic analysis or information technology; others, such as pilots and border agents, are active in the field every day. Many of the available positions, especially for people just beginning their careers, are for support staff members. The duties include record keeping, facilities security, and vehicle maintenance and operation: functions that are performed largely in the background but are vital nonetheless.

THE MAJOR AGENCIES OF DHS

The responsibilities of Homeland Security's twenty-two major agencies and other sections go far beyond those of the four organizations highlighted in this book. Among the others are the following:

Citizenship and Immigration Services (CIS) aids individuals and businesses in resolving issues connected to citizenship and immigration.

Customs and Border Protection (CBP) monitors people and cargo coming into the country, watching for terrorist weapons and enforcing immigration laws at and near borders.

The Domestic Nuclear Detection Office (DNDO) coordinates efforts by federal and local government agencies to provide comprehensive and coordinated policies and plans in the event of a nuclear attack or accident. It also has at the ready Mobile Detection Deployment Units (MDDUs), vehicles with cutting-edge radiation detection instruments.

The Federal Law Enforcement Training Center (FLETC) oversees a network of facilities that provide training to more than eighty interagency law enforcement coalitions and many more individual law enforcement agencies across the country.

The Office of Health Affairs (OHA) coordinates medical activities to make sure DHS is prepared for and able to respond to medical issues that fall within its responsibilities.

The Office of Intelligence and Analysis (I&A) oversees the collection and analysis of information that may affect current or future threats.

The Office of Operations Coordination and Planning (OPS) coordinates DHS activities within the department and with law enforcement agencies around the country.

The Science and Technology Directorate (S&T) is responsible for managing DHS's overall scientific and technological research and development.

The U.S. Secret Service (USSS) safeguards the nation's financial infrastructure and protects national leaders, visiting heads of state and government, and others, especially at certain significant events and places.

JOBS WITHIN CUSTOMS AND BORDER PROTECTION

Obviously, all the many agencies within DHS—not just the four highlighted in this book—provide dozens of opportunities for rewarding careers. For example, Customs and Border Protection (CBP) needs people to perform its primary duty—to enforce immigration and customs laws at and near U.S. borders. This work includes such responsibilities as apprehending people trying to come into the country illegally, with a special emphasis on potential terrorists; stopping the smuggling of weapons, drugs, and other illegal items; making sure that food coming in from other countries meets American standards for consumption and complies with the regulations of the federal Department of Agriculture; and, in general, enforcing U.S. trade laws. All of this must be carried out while at the same time making sure that the flow of goods and products will continue unhindered.

Patrolling the border between the United States and Mexico is a major task for employees of the DHS. Here, border patrol agents apprehend an undocumented worker.

To fulfill these duties, CBP has over 58,000 employees. The bulk of them are agents and officers on the front line, stationed along America's borders. Some are uniformed, while others are in civilian clothes.

If you become a CBP agent or officer, you can expect to work frequently in difficult, harsh, and even dangerous conditions. You will be on duty for long and sometimes irregular periods, and you must be prepared and willing to carry firearms.

In 2011 the job descriptions of five of CBP's main job categories were as follows:

- Agents, who patrol and protect the nearly 2,000 miles (3,218.7 kilometers [km]) of the nation's southern border with Mexico, 5,000 miles (8,046.7 km) of its northern border with Canada, and over 2,000 miles (3,218.8 km) of coastline around Florida, the Gulf of Mexico, and Puerto Rico.

- Officers, who screen passengers, vehicles, aircraft, ships, and cargo arriving at the nation's more than three hundred seaports and airports to detect and detain terrorists and **contraband,** such as weapons of mass destruction, from entering the United States, while maintaining legitimate trade and travel.

- Air and marine **interdiction** agents, who use high-tech equipment to detect (typically from great distances) the entry of undocumented noncitizens, weapons, narcotics, and other contraband.

- Agriculture specialists, who are responsible for halting the spread of pests and diseased animals and plants that pose threats to the nation's farms and food supply.

- Revenue enforcement agents, who enforce trade and **tariff** laws. These agents collect more than $30 billion in entry duties and taxes every year, which is the second-largest revenue source for the federal government. In addition, they fulfill the agency's trade mission by appraising and classifying imported merchandise.

In addition to these jobs and others that are considered primary job categories in CBP, you might want to apply for a position as one of CBP's support employees. Again, the range of support positions is broad, including the following:

- Drone pilots, who operate the unmanned drone aircraft of the Customs and Border Patrol
- Information Technology (IT) specialists, who install, maintain, and operate computer networks
- Intelligence analysts, whose purpose is to develop and use emerging technologies to monitor and analyze threats that may be crossing the U.S. borders
- Intelligence research specialists, who collect and analyze data related to immigration and customs laws
- Mission support specialists, who provide logistical and administrative support to agents during missions
- Paralegals, who assist CPB lawyers in preparing cases

One of the primary DHS agencies is Customs and Border Protection (CBP). Here are some statistics that give an idea of what it does:

- CBP deploys some 1,500 canine enforcement teams, 25,000 automobiles, 300 aircraft, 260 watercraft, and 300 equestrian (horse) patrols daily.
- It covers about 1,900 miles (3057 km) of border with Mexico, 5,000 miles (8046 km) of border with Canada, 330 ports of entry (official entry points), and about 140 Border Patrol stations.
- On a typical day in 2010, CBP
  - Employed about 59,000 people.
  - Made about 2,000 apprehensions of people entering illegally and 75 arrests of criminals.
  - Processed about 965,000 passengers and pedestrians, as well as 47,300 truck, rail, and sea containers.
  - Seized about 11,400 pounds of narcotics and submitted 540 pest interception reports.

- Pilots, who fly the agency's helicopters and airplanes
- Security specialists, who are responsible for such duties as patrolling CBP facilities to ensure the safety of other employees
- Staff in other specialized fields, such as photography, public relations, recruiting, office support, record keeping, economics, engineering, foreign languages, detention, and medicine
- Technical support personnel, mechanics, and other maintenance specialists, who maintain surveillance equipment, vehicles, aircraft, and other tools used by agents

These are just *some* of the jobs offered by *just one* of DHS's twenty-two primary agencies and dozens of smaller divisions. You can find many more by visiting the Homeland Security website (*www.dhs.gov/index.shtm*), the sites of the individual departments, or the official site for positions in the federal government (*www.usajobs.opm.gov/*).

ARE YOU ELIGIBLE FOR A JOB?

If you think you'd like to join DHS, the first step is to make sure you meet its requirements. For obvious reasons, these can—and will—differ greatly depending on the specific agency and the specific job. Being a pilot for Immigration and Customs Enforcement, for example, requires a set of skills unlike those needed to be an engineer in the Coast Guard or a record keeper in Customs and Border Protection. A mechanic who keeps the Secret Service's vehicles in good order does not need the skills required of an airport security employee in the TSA or a FEMA heavy-equipment operator who rescues survivors of earthquakes.

However, all applicants for a position anywhere in Homeland Security must meet certain minimum requirements. For one thing, you have to be a U.S. citizen (native born or naturalized). You must have at least a high school diploma or a GED equivalent. Many (but not all) jobs also require at least a two-year college degree and/or previous experience.

You also have to be willing to be photographed and fingerprinted. For many jobs, you must be able to pass basic physical and mental health tests, be willing to comply with random drug testing and, in some cases, take a polygraph (lie detector) test.

You'll need to be eligible for security clearance as well.

Furthermore, you'll have to be willing and able to pass a background check. In this process the agency will thoroughly examine your life history, looking in particular for such things as felony crime convictions or prior drug use. The background check will also look for financial problems, such as large outstanding loans, since it is important to minimize any reason for an employee to accept a bribe. There will be interviews from your family members, friends, and work colleagues to make sure that you have such personal characteristics as a good work ethic and the ability to take direction and work well—both by yourself and as part of a team.

APPLYING FOR A JOB

Previously, many people who wanted to work for DHS and other federal agencies were frustrated by the tedious process of applying for more than one position at a time. Now, however, the government has simplified and streamlined the application process. (Applying for an internship position with a DHS agency, which is discussed in detail later, is similar to this process.)

The first step is to visit the government's official site for job openings, *www.usajobs.opm.gov/*. There, you'll find links to positions currently open, along with descriptions that provide details on specific requirements, salary, and other aspects of the work. It will also let you register and open an account, so that you can apply for an opening that interests you. You will be able to search by job skill, job description, or physical location.

Additionally, you'll be able to use the site to find the

location of the nearest office for the agency you're interested in. At that office, you'll be able to talk to a recruiter and learn more about the position. You can also check online to find upcoming job fairs in your area, where recruiters will be available to answer questions. Furthermore, you can take advantage of the government's Interactive Voice Response Telephone System, by calling 703-724-1850, or its TDD option at 978-461-8404.

Through your online account, you'll be able to create a single **resumé** that can be used as a template for any government job application. This document, on which you list all the basic information that might be needed, can be easily modified to fit a specific job at any agency. (Local recruiters will be able to guide you through the application process if you choose.) The *usajobs.com* site will even give you valuable tips on how to make sure your application is the best it can possibly be.

Such tips are valuable when you apply for any job, not just one with DHS or another department of the federal government. Among the things to consider:

- Watch the job listings regularly. Positions are always opening up as new jobs are created or people retire or leave jobs. The time period for applying for a particular job is often quite short, so it's important to submit your application as soon as possible after the job has been posted.

- Look carefully at the entire announcement related to the job you are interested in. Ask yourself questions such as: Is it near where I live, or in a location I'd be willing to move to? Do I have enough experience and education to qualify? Will the salary meet my needs? Will I be able to complete my application before the deadline? In other words: Don't waste your time applying for a job you can see you're highly unlikely to get.

- Be thorough. Make sure that you have answered all the questions and provided the required information completely—and then some. Do you speak another language? Have you had extensive computer experience? If so, be sure to say that.

- Don't be afraid to brag a little—but not too much!—about your accomplishments and qualifications. It's important to present yourself professionally, and in the best possible light, without overdoing it or sounding egotistical.

- Pay attention to grammar and spelling, and think things through carefully as you write. The way you express yourself counts because the agencies you are applying to will be looking for detail-oriented people who can present their thoughts clearly.

- Keep it short. You want to express yourself fully, but as briefly as possible. Recruiters receive far more applications than they can seriously consider, and a cover letter that is eloquent but concise will catch their attention much more easily than one that is chatty and long-winded.

- So you should ask yourself: Will the recruiter be able to see quickly if I meet the basic requirements? Is the same true for my credentials—that is, the points that make me well qualified? Is the most important information easily found and at the beginning? In short: Don't bury the best points way down in your application.

- Keep it simple. Avoid too much complexity. Recruiters are busy people who don't need to know every detail of your life. At least during this first part of the process, their main concern lies in the qualifications that relate specifically to the job you're hoping to get.

Once you've submitted your application, the next move is up to the agency. If your application demonstrates that you meet the basic requirements, your paperwork will be forwarded to the appropriate hiring official. Typically, you will then be interviewed in person or on the phone. If you make a good impression, you'll be asked to come in for more interviews and testing.

The entire application and hiring process is carefully regulated to ensure fairness for everyone. As with all federal agencies, DHS complies with laws forbidding discrimination on the basis of race, color, religion, sex, sexual orientation, or national origin. Similarly, if you have a disability, Homeland Security recruiters will take it into account and will observe all relevant federal regulations and policies.

If you meet all the DHS requirements, as well as all the requirements for the specific position, you're another step closer to a career with one of Homeland Security's many organizations. If you submit a great application and make a good impression when you meet the recruiter, that's another step to being hired for the job you want.

TWO

TRANSPORTATION SECURITY ADMINISTRATION

ANYONE WHO'S FLOWN ON AN AIRPLANE SINCE 9/11 has gone through security checks at the airport. These checks provide the opportunity for trained individuals to look at passengers and their carry-on bags, making sure that nothing that could endanger travelers is allowed on board the aircraft.

It has become routine for people who go through security procedures to complain—sometimes loudly—about the time the checks take and the hassles they create. On the other hand, most travelers understand how important the checks are—that is, how crucial it is to maintain safety in the skies.

That's where the Transportation Security Administration (TSA) comes in. Its job is complex, but its goal is simple: to protect travelers and flight crews from potential danger. The public faces of the TSA—the people you see when you go through airport security—are only some of the men and women of the agency, and airports are only some of the places

The Transportation Security Administration is tasked with making airports as secure as can be. When full-body scanners were introduced in 2010, many complained about the invasion of privacy but most passengers opted to go through the scanners in the name of national security.

they serve. Everyone in the TSA, however, works to make that goal of travel safety a reality for passengers and crew.

FOCUSING ON SAFETY FOR AIR TRAVELERS

By tradition, U.S. borders have always been more open than those of many other countries. However, the terrorist attacks of 9/11 dramatically increased the need to make sure those borders remain safe, while at the same time maintaining as much of the country's open policy as possible. Part of this effort means ensuring that all people who cross a U.S. border, whether they're entering or leaving the country, will be protected from harm. The TSA was established with this in mind.

The TSA was born in the period following the terrorist attacks of 9/11, during the same period as the formation of the overall division of Homeland Security. The U.S. government

federally operated organization to monitor air travel. Previously, individual passenger airline companies had had this responsibility.

Soon after its formation, the TSA expanded to include other forms of transport, such as mass transit and trains. However, air travel is still the TSA's primary responsibility. As a result, airports make up the area of security most closely associated by the public with the TSA.

The organization has many specific jobs related to its air-safety duties. Among the most important are the following:

- Checking travel documents such as boarding passes and personal identification
- Patrolling sensitive areas to minimize the chances of unauthorized people tampering with baggage and cargo
- Screening passengers and baggage for objects that could be used as weapons
- Using bomb-detecting equipment to monitor cargo

Performing well in these and the other air-related jobs of the TSA is an enormous responsibility and requires a large workforce. As of early 2011, the agency employed nearly 60,000 people to protect some 460 airports around the country. (The agency does not operate in all airports because some facilities prefer to hire private security companies, though they too must meet TSA standards.)

The nation's commercial air fleet is made up of about 6,000

airliners, with roughly 30,000 flights taking off and landing each day. The Airline Pilots Security Alliance estimates that as of 2011 some 800 million passengers traveled by air every year in the nation's air transportation system—and that number is expected to rise.

All told, the TSA employees who work at airports monitor about 2 million air passengers a day—not to mention the passengers' baggage and other cargo the planes are carrying. Because of this huge volume of traffic, the TSA is not able to monitor every aspect of all air traffic in the United States. However, it does provide service for the majority of people flying from U.S. airports, either domestically or internationally. According to TSA estimates, as of early 2011 about 85 percent of these travelers fly on planes where every passenger, crew member, and item of baggage and cargo has been screened.

SOME OF TSA'S JOBS

Since the TSA's overall transportation security work is such a huge responsibility, and the agency employs so many people, it has been divided into subagencies, each of which contains a broad spectrum of specific jobs. Consider, for example, just the people who work in the organization's airport-related segment. Some of the categories these employees fill are explained here.

TRANSPORTATION SECURITY OFFICERS (TSOs)

The largest single segment of TSA's employees, about 50,000 in all as of 2011, work as transportation security officers at airports. To the public, TSOs are the most familiar of all the agency's employees. They are the people on duty when you

NO FROZEN MONKEY HEADS, PLEASE

Even after years of being told about prohibited items, air travelers still sometimes try to bring dangerous items along—including unusual weapons such as nunchucks, throwing stars, and swords concealed inside canes. One passenger tried to get through security with a fully gassed-up chainsaw.

Sometimes you will see things that are just pretty weird. Here are a few items that have turned up:

A suitcase full of cockroaches

A drugged tiger cub hidden among stuffed toys

Seventy-five snakes hidden in a woman's bra

Ninety-five boa constrictors—so many that the bag they were hidden in burst on the conveyor belt

More than a dozen live songbirds strapped to a passenger's legs

Two live pigeons concealed under tights, worn by a man under his pants

A dead cat stuffed with drugs

Seven pounds of chocolate-coated heroin bars

Drugs concealed in canned vegetables, liquor bottles, sets of dentures, and many more items

$1.2 million in diamonds, found on a passenger who said he had nothing to declare

Corpses, brought through security on wheelchairs, probably to avoid paying a fee for transporting a dead body

And then there was that frozen monkey head . . .

pass through security checks on your way to boarding a plane.

TSOs fill a number of vital roles. For example, they examine travel documents, using black light and magnifying devices to check for forgeries. With the assistance of X-ray machines, wands, and other **noninvasive** devices, TSOs also screen all passengers and their bags. If necessary, TSOs perform individual pat-downs. They also monitor key points leading to and from secure areas in airports.

As a TSO, it is possible that you would rotate positions and take on other duties, many of which are carried out behind the scenes. For example, you might be responsible for monitoring other TSA workers. This means that instead of focusing on travelers, you would randomly visit various points around the airport to make sure that other employees are abiding by the rules and doing their jobs well.

The purpose of monitoring TSA colleagues, of course, is to make sure that everyone is maintaining strict security procedures. Such procedures include entering restricted areas safely, displaying identity badges prominently, and in general watching out for possible security threats. If you are a roving inspector, you might also be assigned to monitor service vehicles (such as food service trucks) and employees' cars as they enter and leave the airport.

TRANSPORTATION SECURITY INSPECTORS (TSIs)

In some ways, transportation security inspectors have duties that resemble those of TSOs. The main difference is the scale at which TSIs monitor situations: instead of keeping an eye on security procedures that relate to individual passengers or specific areas of airports, they monitor broader cargo and passenger systems.

For example, as a TSI you might be assigned to inspect cargo warehouses or more extensive portions of an airport, searching for weaknesses in the overall security of those systems. Another position you might fill as a TSI involves making sure that cargo companies, food service companies, and other large private organizations are complying with all TSA regulations within the airport.

BEHAVIOR DETECTION OFFICERS (BDOs)

Behavior detection officers (BDOs) have a very special and sensitive mission. Rather than physically inspecting passengers as they move through security checkpoints, BDOs are trained to inconspicuously observe what passengers are doing: how they behave.

The purpose of this observation is to identify passengers or other visitors to the airport who may be potential threats. Typically, such persons arouse suspicions because they exhibit unusual behavior, such as excessive nervousness or erratic movements that may indicate a risk of criminal intent. If there is sufficient reason, a BDO can ask the passenger to step out of the security line for further screening. The BDO may also ask for help from police officers in escorting the passenger aside for further questioning.

Part of the training process to be a BDO is learning to evaluate subtle differences in a situation. Is someone really a potential threat, or just a little nervous about flying? Another very important part of your training will be to avoid profiling—that is, singling out individuals based solely on apparent race, ethnicity, or religion.

As the name indicates, Explosives Detection Canine Teams (EDCTs) use dogs that have been specially trained to sniff out the presence of dangerous explosives. The canines selected for this work typically come from breeds well known for their intelligence and sensitive noses—for example, German shepherds, Belgian Malinois, and Vizslas.

Most of the TSA's roughly 450 canine teams are stationed at airports. However, some are assigned to patrol other transportation systems, such as mass transit, that in certain areas are considered to be high-risk targets for bombs.

If you join an EDCT, you might sometimes be deployed to work in places outside the usual TSA system. For example, you

Cargo inspector Sachin Vaidya shows his TSA dog how to inspect airport cargo.

might from time to time help other federal agencies, such as the Department of State or the Secret Service. Requests for this kind of help typically mean that the canine teams are needed to provide extra security for, say, a public appearance by a high-profile political figure. EDCTs are also often called on to help in emergency situations, such as bomb threats in schools or office buildings.

FEDERAL AIR MARSHALS (FAMs)

If TSOs are the public face of air transportation security, and TSIs, BDOs, and EDCTs are somewhat less conspicuous, then members of the Federal Air Marshal Service (FAMS) are at the opposite end of the spectrum. They try to be invisible. As an air marshal, your job will depend on blending in with passengers and remaining anonymous.

FAMs are the TSA's primary law enforcement unit. They are armed plainclothes officers who travel on commercial flights, both within the United States and overseas, as if they were ordinary passengers.

If you become an FAM, your mission will be to spot possible criminals or terrorists who may have targeted aircraft, airports, passengers, or crew members. In a 2005 article in the *Washington Post*, Federal Air Marshal Service official Patrick F. Sullivan stated that air marshals "are trained to covertly detect potential criminal terrorist pre-attack surveillance and other suspicious activity."

The Federal Air Marshal Service is an elite team that is extremely difficult to get into. For one thing, as an FAM you will need to learn and maintain a number of very specific skills, such as the use of weapons and defensive techniques in the close quarters of an aircraft. Because of these requirements, those chosen to become air marshals are typically seasoned professionals from law enforcement agencies.

The job is obviously difficult and potentially dangerous, especially since the number of marshals on duty is relatively small. Prior to 9/11, there were only thirty-three FAMs on active duty. Today, the TSA says that they number in the thousands, although exact figures on how many officers are active at a given time are confidential.

Even with this increase in active marshals, the Federal Air Marshal Service can cover only a fraction of the flights that come in and out of the nation's airports. It is estimated that only about 5 percent of flights include an FAM as a passenger, even when the figure calculated includes the growing number of pilots who also are armed when on duty.

TECHNOLOGY

Depending on your specific job within the TSA, you may use a variety of high-tech tools. For example, if you are a TSO you will routinely use X-ray machines and handheld metal-detecting wands to make sure that passengers don't board a plane with concealed weapons. Such machines aren't new, but the need for them has skyrocketed since 9/11, and they are constantly being updated and improved.

Other examples of cutting-edge technology are used in the science of **biometrics**. Techniques of biometrics allow security officers to verify the identity of a passenger or worker. The TSA is currently testing a number of advances in biometric

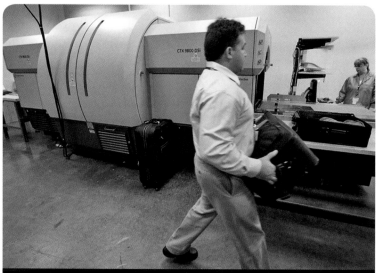

TSA workers use a variety of high-tech tools. Here, a technician carries a suitcase containing a simulated hidden explosive to a computed tomography scanning machine that can almost instantly create a complete three-dimensional X-ray image.

technology, such as the use of e-passports, which store photos, fingerprints, and other data on microchips embedded in these travel documents.

Another tool you might use for screening travelers is called advanced imaging technology (AIT), developed because many passengers object to the use of standard X-ray machines and other forms of screening. Many believe that the standard machines violate passengers' privacy, since much of a person's body can be seen on the projected image.

AIT addresses this concern by displaying a passenger's image on a monitor that is viewed by a TSO in a separate room. If you are the officer using this technology, you will not directly see the passenger, and his or her facial image will be blurred.

"LADY GAGA'S HANDCUFFS"

Many air passengers are confused about what they can and cannot bring on airplanes. For example, knitting needles are permitted. So are corkscrews without knives. Nail clippers, contrary to common belief, are also acceptable.

To help answer questions about items that might not be okay, TSA has an app, My TSA, for mobile devices and on the Web. My TSA has a tool called "Can I Bring My…"

Enter the name of the item you're curious about, and the tool will tell you if it's okay to bring it. In general, being specific will help. Here are a few tips for using "Can I Bring My . . . " effectively:

Don't type just the word "food"—that's too vague. Be more specific: brownie, apple, pudding.

But don't be too specific, or the app won't pick up keywords. For example, you don't need to name the brand name of, say, a deodorant, but you do need to identify whether it's roll-on or stick. The same applies to the inclusion of a specific number of items—"disposable razor" will do the trick, but not "two" or "three" disposable razors.

Of course, most of what TSA employees see in X-ray searches is quite harmless. Sometimes they find dangerous items, though, such as weapons or fireworks.

And sometimes they find some very unusual things. "Blogger Bob," who writes for TSA's website, had this to say about one such oddball carry-on:

You may have heard about Lady Gaga recently being permitted to take handcuffs through a checkpoint at LAX [Los Angeles International Airport]. Some [travelers] assumed handcuffs were prohibited, and were very surprised to find out they're not. Why not, you might ask? They're not a threat. You can't do any real damage with a pair of handcuffs and if you really wanted to tie someone's hands behind their back, there are many other ways you could do it. I'm sure you're thinking of a few right now.

Find My TSA app at
http://itunes.apple.com/us/app/my-tsa/id380200364?mt=8

This ensures that a TSO will not be able to recognize a passenger later who has already been seen "naked."

Another example of technology that you might use at a security checkpoint is a procedure called explosives trace detection (ETD). The ETD procedure is used to randomly screen carry-on baggage and passengers. TSO employees assigned to ETD duty use special swabs to detect tiny traces of explosives that may be clinging to baggage or to people's hands.

EXPERIMENTAL SCREENING TECHNOLOGY

In its ongoing effort to improve airport security measures, TSA is experimenting with a wide range of new devices. One, for example, if put into use, would blow puffs of air at passengers to loosen, collect, and identify any tiny particles of explosive residue.

Another new and experimental tool is called Cast-Scope. A modified form of X-ray technology, CastScope is specifically designed to scan casts, leg braces, heavy bandages, and **prosthetic** limbs. The machine does this through the use of backscatter X rays, which have an important difference from medical X rays. Whereas medical X rays pass completely through the body, backscatter X rays penetrate only about a quarter-inch beneath the surface they contact, yet provide a clear image of what's below it.

The machines are thus especially useful in situations where alarms on standard X-ray machines would be set off by, say, the metal parts of a brace or prosthetic. CastScope allows hidden areas to be screened without drawing unwanted attention to people with medical conditions.

SUPPORT PERSONNEL

In addition to the major categories of jobs that are well known, there are dozens of others within the TSA to consider. These positions are typically filled by skilled professionals and provide vital support for the administration's various security activities. As the agency's website notes, it "needs your professional, technical, or administrative talents to support the mission of protecting the skies." If you take a job with TSA, these jobs won't be available to you right away. They require years of experience and training. However, you will be able to apply for them in time whether you have been working for the organization or elsewhere.

As an example of these professional positions, numerous support jobs must be filled to maintain just one part of the TSA: the Federal Air Marshal Service. Clearly, the flying marshals require extensive support networks on the ground in order to succeed. A few of the many different support positions that the service requires are listed in the following subsections:

INTELLIGENCE OFFICERS

Intelligence officers specialize in the collection, analysis, evaluation, and distribution of information from a variety of sources originating both within the United States and abroad. This information is collected because it may indicate a threat. Air marshals then use the data to pinpoint potential dangers.

INSTRUCTORS

FAMS instructors have extensive experience in a variety of specialized fields. Their job is to conduct workshops and trainings for airline crew members and others in the field. This process provides the students with knowledge and hands-on experience in self-defense, crisis negotiation, and other procedures and techniques they may need.

INFORMATION TECHNOLOGY (IT) AND TECHNOLOGY SPECIALISTS

IT specialists are experts in developing, installing, and maintaining the agency's computer technology. Similarly, experts are also needed to develop and maintain other forms of technology, such as advanced communications devices. These technology systems are vital to maintaining an accurate and speedy flow of information among air marshals who are on duty and members of the FAMS who are on the ground.

In addition to positions such as these, the Federal Air Marshal Service employs a wide range of other support personnel. They handle duties such as maintaining records and assisting in office-based security operations, as well as being responsible for administrative office work and other assistance.

REQUIREMENTS AND TRAINING

The basics that you need to be able to apply for a job with the TSA are similar to those in other parts of the Department of Homeland Security. For example, you must be a U.S. citizen with at least a high school diploma or a GED equivalent. You must be willing to be photographed and fingerprinted, and you'll have to pass both physical and mental health tests. Undergoing a background check, agreeing to random drug testing, and submitting to other measures are likewise similar to requirements found elsewhere in DHS.

The requirements beyond the basics will depend on the specific job. As with most kinds of employment, within Homeland Security and elsewhere, you'll need training before you can begin work. Again, the specifics of your training will depend on the particular job.

For example, the basic training for a Transportation Security Officer, the most commonly held TSA job, includes about 130 hours of study, roughly half of them devoted to acquiring hands-on experience. During your training period, you'll learn how to handle a variety of situations you can expect to encounter.

You will also learn specific skills, such as the ability to recognize improvised explosive devices (IEDs) hidden in luggage and clothing. TSOs as a group view some 45,000 X-ray images of dangerous and prohibited items daily. Obviously, recognizing such items quickly is a vital skill—as is dealing with any you spot. Perhaps just as important is learning the difference between a potential hazard and, say, a can of shaving cream that is genuinely just a can of shaving cream.

At the same time, you'll learn about the importance of personal interactions—that is, relating well to the travelers you will encounter. After all, you're about to become the public face of the TSA, so you need to act with appropriate professionalism. Your training will thus emphasize the importance of friendliness, respect, politeness, and other elements of professional behavior. In addition, you'll get instruction in handling potential hazards.

In addition to your initial training as a TSO, you will be required to attend periodic refresher classes while on the job. You can expect to spend fifty to sixty hours a year attending these classes to help you review what you already know and receive instruction on new techniques, tools, and policies.

Some TSA jobs, meanwhile, call for training much more extensive than what is required of a TSO. For example, if you are chosen to be part of a canine team, you will attend classes at the Transportation Security Administration's canine training facilities in San Antonio, Texas. There, you will be paired with a four-legged partner, who will have already undergone extensive training. Both of you will then take part in an intensive, ten-week course that will turn you into a close and thoroughly bonded team.

OUTSIDE THE AIRPORT

When the Transportation Security Administration was formed in 2001, its responsibilities were confined to airports and commercial aircraft. Soon after that, the Department of Homeland Security recognized the need to make all forms of transportation secure. It therefore expanded TSA's role to include other aspects of transportation as well. In a 2005 article in the *Washington Post*, David Adams, a spokesman for the agency, commented:

> TSA is going to extend its outreach into other modes of transportation. We think this is a very good approach to test our tools and quickly deploy resources in the

event of a situation or a threat. It shows we could be at any of these places.

This statement signals that, in addition to jobs in airport security, there are thousands of additional jobs within the Transportation Security Administration that need to be filled. This is because the TSA is also responsible for keeping travelers and cargo safe on the nation's most heavily used bus systems, railroads, mass transit lines, ferries, and port facilities.

One of the main ways the TSA secures these systems is through the use of roving groups called Visible Intermodal Prevention and Response (VIPR) teams. These teams are made up of representatives from several different specialized groups, including FAMs, TSOs, TSIs, BDOs, and EDCTs. These employees of the federal TSA work in conjunction with local security and law enforcement officers.

Some members of VIPR teams wear jackets bearing the TSA name on the back, to identify them as security agents. However, others are in plainclothes so that they can blend in with civilian passengers. In the *Washington Post* article, spokesman Adams commented about these anonymous agents: "The whole purpose [of the program] is that people will not know when we're going to be there or [even] if we are going to be there. It's a preventative approach."

In addition to the main focus of their work, TSA employees are responsible for a number of other duties. Some of these concern various aspects of the flow of materials in and out of the country. A little-known responsibility for TSA, for instance, is providing security for the nation's complex system of pipe-lines. The TSA monitors some 160,000 miles (257,000 km) of pipelines that carry hazardous liquids, 310,000 miles (500,000 km) of oil pipelines, and a whopping 2 million miles (3.2 million km) of natural gas pipelines.

Needless to say, still more jobs are available within the agency for security agents to patrol these systems. Since pipe-line systems are often in remote locations, anyone who works in this area of TSA's duties needs to be prepared for, and com-fortable with, assignments in rugged conditions.

SALARIES AND BENEFITS

As is true within the entire Department of Homeland Security, TSA employees are federal workers and are paid according to a set of guidelines called the General Services (GS) Schedule. The GS has fifteen pay grades, and within each grade are ten steps. Each of these grades, and each step within them, has a specified salary level. Your salary will thus be determined by where you are on the scale; moving up depends on such factors as senior-ity, the level of responsibility, and the difficulty of your job.

The pay TSA employees receive covers a broad range. A highly trained professional, such as a specialist in information technology, can expect an appropriately high salary. Depend-ing on location, experience, and other factors, an IT specialist with the administration received an annual base salary in 2011 of about $57,000 to $70,000.

The majority of employees within the Transportation Secu-rity Administration, however, earn lower salaries. For example, as of 2011 the starting salary for a TSO was $25,518 to $38,277 per year. However, this is what is called a base salary. Employees are typically eligible for higher pay if they work in regions with higher living expenses, and pay raises can come quickly.

Meanwhile, full-time TSA employees are eligible for an array of benefits, which, like salaries, are determined by federal guidelines. These benefits include health and life insurance, retirement and pension plans, and sick leave and vacation days. Smaller benefits, such as uniform allowances and public transportation vouchers, are typically included as well.

In addition to these overall benefits and salary packages, the TSA has several programs designed to make their employees' jobs better and more fulfilling. For example, the Career Evolution Program supports promotions for people who join at entry-level positions. This boosts the chances that high-quality and valued employees will remain within the TSA for many years.

Another job incentive is a pay-for-performance program. This system provides pay raises and bonuses for employees who do outstanding work. Furthermore, TSA provides special bonuses for certain employees. For example, since the canine members of explosives-sniffing teams typically live with their human partners, if you're a dog handler you will receive extra pay to compensate for the animal's care and feeding.

THREE

IMMIGRATION AND CUSTOMS ENFORCEMENT

THEY STOP THE SMUGGLING OF EVERYTHING FROM drugs to weapons, from counterfeit money to rare animals. They break up illegal immigration operations. They investigate the import and export of unapproved substances. They curb illegal gambling offshore. They deport convicted foreign criminals who are hiding in the United States. They enforce laws about human rights violations and financial crimes. They dismantle international criminal organizations. They investigate crimes connected to art theft, international gang activities, and identity fraud.

That's just part of what the members of the Immigration and Customs Enforcement (ICE) team do. Like other components of Homeland Security, ICE was formed after 9/11 as the result of merging three existing organizations that focused on issues of immigration and customs. ICE is the second largest law enforcement agency in the country, topped only by the FBI.

The ICE police have grown to have an enormous role in protecting our nation's security.

Today ICE is responsible for investigating and enforcing violations of over four hundred separate federal laws. Each of these laws focuses on a specific aspect of the nation's borders, immigration policies, customs, transportation, and infrastructure.

As of early 2011, ICE had between 15,000 and 20,000 employees in the United States and overseas. There are four law enforcement divisions working out of many offices across the country, with a particular emphasis on the United States–Mexico border. The ICE facilities include detention and processing centers, field offices, and support offices.

HOMELAND SECURITY INVESTIGATIONS

A key part of ICE is Homeland Security Investigations (HSI). Roughly half of ICE's employees work in HSI. HSI's primary focus is on the issue that is the one most people know about:

upholding immigration laws. Enforcing these laws is a daunt-ing task. On any given day, more than 30,000 people who are not U.S. citizens are being held in detention in over two hun-dred detention centers, jails, and prisons nationwide. (Non-citizens are sometimes referred to as "aliens." This term can simply mean "noncitizens." However, the word is also consid-ered by many people to be derogatory.) They are awaiting the conclusions of trials determining the disposition of their cases.

Some of them may have entered and remained in the United States illegally. Some are in the country legally but are suspected of having committed crimes. And some may be involved in threats to national security. If convicted, the person will be deported to his or her home country.

HSI is responsible for much more than cases of illegal immigration. The agency is also responsible for investigating and following through on a wide variety of other criminal activities, including human rights violations; the smuggling of humans, narcotics, weapons, and other contraband (such as pirated software and CDs); international fraud and financial crimes (such as the counterfeiting of currency); and cyber-crime. As the HSI website states, "If it's a crime involving a person, commodity, or money illegally entering or leaving the United States, HSI investigates it."

One of the most important aspects of this work is the moni-toring of the vast amounts of cargo that pass across the nation's borders and through its ports by land, sea, and air. This is another massive job: it is estimated that each year more than 11 million containers of goods arrive at U.S. seaports, with another 14 million coming into the country by truck and rail.

TOOLS OF THE TRADE

To help them in their work, ICE agents have a number of tools at their disposal. For example, they usually carry handguns and may sometimes also be issued shoulder firearms such as shotguns, rifles, or carbines. Like all federal and local law enforcement agencies, HSI officers follow very strict guidelines when handling or using their weapons.

HSI officers often use other tools as well. For example, they can employ airplanes, helicopters, and other forms of transportation if necessary.

Fingerprint analysis and other areas of forensic science are also integral tools of the trade for the agency. Customs inspection agents have at their disposal technology such as X-ray, gamma-imaging, and radiation detection systems.

Furthermore, ICE operates a nationwide radio communication system: the National Law Enforcement Communications Center (NLECC), based in Orlando, Florida. Designed especially for ICE, this system allows ICE agents and officers to communicate with one another easily and quickly across the United States.

HSI PROFESSIONALS

Most of the cargo that passes across U.S. borders is a legitimate part of the nation's commerce—but not all of it. So when there's a suspicion of smuggling or illegal importation of contraband, ICE begins an investigation and, if necessary, apprehends the criminals.

The primary investigators on these cases are called special agents. To the public, they are the most familiar figures of ICE—the ones in the jackets marked ICE who frequently appear in the news media. However, special agents could not

As part of an ongoing effort to stop the influx of illegal immigrants, border fences such as this one near San Diego, California, have been constructed all along the border of the United States and Mexico.

operate without a large team of professionals and other support staff members backing them up.

So there are many other positions that need to be filled within the agency. One of HSI's main divisions, the Office of Intelligence, requires the expertise of professionals who are, as the agency's name indicates, highly skilled in the field of intelligence. Within this office, research specialists focus on analyzing data that has been collected on a given case, so that it can be used by ICE's agents who are in the field. As with other specialized professionals, a highly focused position such as this is typically filled by someone with some years of experience, education, and training. However, an entry-level position, or an internship with the agency, can be an excellent means of working your way into the job. Often, if you have an entry-level position in the same general field of work, you can study and be trained for it while getting on-the-job experience at the same time.

Raw **intelligence data** comes from many law enforcement agencies and other sources around the world. So, to do its work effectively, the Office of Intelligence works closely with other government agencies, including the Central Intelligence

Agency, the Federal Bureau of Investigation, U.S. Customs and Border Protection, and their overseas counterparts.

Another major component of ICE is its Office of Enforcement and Removal Operations (ERO). This organization's primary employees are called immigration enforcement agents (IEAs). If you become an IEA, among your duties will be to aid in the investigation, identification, tracing, and arrest of people who are not lawfully in the country. You will also oversee the physical removal of and care for convicted persons prior to their deportation to their countries of citizenship.

Another branch of ERO is made up of deportation officers (DOs), whose duties often mesh closely with those of IEAs. As a DO, you will be more concerned with legal and logistical matters, monitoring deportation cases as they move through the court systems. You will also supervise individuals who have been released from custody but may still be deported, and you will assist in the prosecution of persons who were deported but have reentered the country illegally.

Frequently, HSI agents and support staff are organized into highly specialized teams, and you might be assigned to one of these. You may be stationed overseas to work with a variety of international law enforcement task forces, **INTERPOL**, and other outside agencies, for example.

One of these specialized international organizations is called the Border Enforcement Security Task Force (BEST). It includes law enforcement professionals from several different nations, including Mexico, Canada, Argentina, and Colombia. Its purpose is to provide cross-border cooperation on cases involving the smuggling of drugs, weapons, and money.

ERO BY THE NUMBERS

One of ICE's divisions, Enforcement and Removal Operations (ERO), is responsible for overseeing the removal of aliens (as ICE often refers to noncitizens) who pose a threat to national security or public safety. To do its job, the agency routinely carries out a wide variety of tasks. Here's a sample of what ERO did on an average day in 2011:

ERO managed 6 Service Processing Centers, oversaw 7 contract detention facilities, and housed aliens in over 240 facilities.

ERO housed an average of 33,384 illegal aliens in these various facilities nationwide, for an average of about 29 days each.

ERO personnel managed over 1.69 million aliens in the various stages of immigration removal proceedings.

ERO processed 1,177 aliens into detention centers.

ERO health care professionals conducted approximately 628 intake health care screenings in facilities staffed by ERO health care providers.

ERO facilitated 298 physical examinations, 94 dental examinations, 355 chronic disease interventions, and 156 mental health interventions.

Facility clinics received 439 detainees during sick call and 903 prescriptions were filled at facilities staffed by ERO health care providers.

Health care personnel saw 41 detainees for urgent care, and there were 46 emergency room or off-site referrals.

Detainees placed 25,379 phone calls.

ERO employees procured 221 travel documents.

ERO removed 1,057 aliens from the United States, including 533 criminal aliens.

Seventeen children were placed with the Office of Refugee Resettlement in the Department of Health and Human Services.

ERO officers arrested 108 fugitive and nonfugitive aliens, many of whom had been convicted for a multitude of crimes.

SUPPORT POSITIONS

ICE has dozens of other positions that you might be qualified to fill. For example, the agency employs personnel called investigative assistants (IAs), who support lead investigators in their work. If you become an IA, you'll be responsible for such duties as gathering data and evidence, conducting inquiries and interviews, researching cases, and preparing background materials for court cases.

IAs don't just work in the background. During active investigations, they are also in the field to support their lead investigators. In this capacity, they carry out such duties as monitoring radio or telephone communication, coordinating other forms of communication when normal means are not possible, responding to urgent requests for information, and developing and using contacts in law enforcement agencies outside ICE to coordinate efforts.

Another of the many career options to choose from if you want a career in ICE is that of technical enforcement officer (TEO). TEOs are specialists in installing, using, and maintaining the varied high-tech equipment used by investigators and other agency personnel. You might be assigned to stay in one location, maintaining equipment and acting as a center for far-flung operations. But you might also need to be in the field on occasion, taking care of the setup and operation of electronic surveillance gear.

Meanwhile, detention and removal assistants (DRAs) fulfill duties that are primarily in offices rather than the field. These include such tasks as compiling and maintaining files on non-citizens who have been detained, as well as reviewing and

Border Patrol Agent John Fogle fingerprints Margarita Lopez after she and her six-year-old son were detained in Nogales, Arizona, for trying to cross the border illegally.

analyzing cases to help administrators decide how to proceed. DRAs also help with the planning and logistics of deporting people who have been convicted of being in the United States illegally. The DRA position is an example of jobs within the agency that do not require a college degree. However, being a DRA is not a position for someone who is just starting a career in the workplace. It, and some other jobs within ICE, typically require you to have a year of experience at a lower-level government job beforehand.

Still another important position is that of language specialist, or linguist. The ability to communicate clearly with those who don't speak English is a vital one for an agency that routinely deals with people from other nations. Because of this need, employees who are fluent in a wide range of languages are in high demand.

As in other agencies, language specialists are called on to interpret in ongoing operations, sometimes in the field and sometimes in ICE offices. They also translate documents, testify or interpret in court, and perform other duties related to their specialty. Sometimes, these are part-time or occasional, on-call positions. Of course, if you are an agent who is fluent in a foreign language, you might be called on to act as a linguist on occasion, in addition to your regular duties.

Among the other positions you might consider as you look forward to a career in ICE after your college training are those in medicine, such as physician, physician's assistant, lab technician, nurse, or social worker. ICE needs to fill these positions because the agency maintains its own teams of health professionals. These teams are trained to handle medical conditions that might arise among detainees. Mental health professionals are also important members of these teams. People who have been detained and are awaiting trial, especially if the wait has been a long one, are naturally stressed and distraught. Many have been separated from family members, have trouble communicating, don't know what the future will bring, are worried about persecution if they return home, or have other serious problems. As a result, detainees often have mental health issues such as depression.

There are still other job possibilities within the ICE organization. As in any large company or organization, for instance, the agency's responsibilities require people to work in many different areas of management and logistics. Among these are offices that focus on budget, finance, human resources, training coordination, legal matters, recruitment, public affairs, building security, and property and equipment maintenance.

STUDENT JOBS AND INTERNSHIPS

If any of these jobs sound appealing, and if you think you might be interested in a career with ICE, you can find out about the agency firsthand by taking part in one of its programs for students and interns. (Many other government agencies have similar programs. You can find out more about these by visiting www.usajobs.gov/ei/studentcareerexperience.asp or www.studentjobs.gov)

As a general rule, you are eligible to apply for one of these programs if you meet certain minimum requirements. These include being a U.S. citizen at least sixteen years old, and being able to obtain and hold a security clearance. (In the United States, security clearance includes a background check and other procedures to verify that you are qualified to hold a sensitive government job.) Beyond those basics, each of the specific programs has other requirements.

For example, the Student Career Experience Program (SCEP) has certain minimum educational requirements. SCEP is a 640-hour course of work and study that typically runs at least one summer, full time; there is part-time work during the school year, as well. To be eligible for SCEP, you need to be enrolled in (or accepted to) an accredited high school, technical, vocational, two- or four-year college or university, or graduate or professional school. You'll also need to maintain a C average or better in a field of study related to your career goals. (Up to half of these required hours may be waived for students who have a GPA of 3.5 or higher.)

Another learning curriculum ICE sponsors is a work-study program called the Student Temporary Employment Program (STEP). STEP is in some ways a more flexible program than SCEP. This is because the work and study you do at ICE, whether part time or full time, doesn't have to be related directly to your academic studies. STEP appointments generally last for up to one year, but typically you will have an opportunity to extend that period if you continue taking at least a half-time course load in school.

Both STEP and SCEP programs offer salaries and certain benefits while you are enrolled. While they don't guarantee that you'll have a job when you graduate, there is a possibility that your student job can be converted to a permanent position when you finish.

ICE also maintains the Student Volunteer Program (SVP). As the name suggests, the program provides students with unpaid opportunities for training and work experience related to their academic studies outside ICE. Like the agency's paid student programs, it's an excellent way to explore a career while honing your personal and professional skills. Furthermore, depending on the specifics of your school, you may be able to get class credit for your participation in the program.

HOW TO APPLY

You don't have to go through one of ICE's student programs to apply for a job with the agency. If you have not been in SCEP or STEP or the SVP, visit the ICE website: www.ice.gov/ as your first step in applying for a position. There, you can see how to find the ICE field office nearest your home.

Ask to speak to a recruitment officer there. He or she will be able to give you more details, including what to expect during the application process. If you decide to continue, the recruiter will also help you through the next stages of the application process.

At that point, you'll go online to see what jobs are available. Like other federal agencies, ICE lists all its open positions on usajobs.gov, the official website of the U.S. Office of Personnel Management. These listings are constantly updated as vacancies open and new positions are added.

Unsurprisingly, beyond the basics required for any job with DHS—minimum age and education, citizenship, and so on—the requirements for specific positions vary. For example, to be eligible to become a technical enforcement officer, you'll need extensive working knowledge and skill in installing, maintaining, and using computers, surveillance, and other technology. In addition, the ability to teach agents to use this equipment is an important part of the job, so you'll need good communication and teaching skills.

Some other jobs also require very specific abilities. For example, if you are applying for a job as a linguist/translator, you will need to be fluent in at least one language besides English. To be an ICE special agent or investigative assistant, meanwhile, you will need either four years of college or a certain minimum amount of experience in law enforcement or a related field. Furthermore, to become a special agent you will have to meet minimum requirements for physical fitness.

(These tests are so strict that many candidates never get further in the application process.)

The requirements for previous work experience vary according to the position. Eligibility for some positions, such as being a pilot, calls for professional licensing and several years of work experience. On the other hand, to be a DRA you need only one year of experience in a related field.

The specifics of the job you apply for will determine, in large part, what will happen as you move through the hiring process. For example, the testing for becoming a special agent, as befits one of ICE's elite jobs, is one of the more stringent within the agency. Overall, however, the application and testing processes will resemble those of other agencies in DHS: oral and written tests, background checks, mental and physical health examination, and other forms of evaluation.

The mental health component is especially important. Every day ICE personnel see people who are desperate, distraught, confused, or possibly dangerous. Furthermore, although ICE personnel typically work together, sometimes they carry out jobs on their own. So it is important that people who work for ICE have the ability to perform both solo and as part of a team. They need to have a knack for defusing tense situations and handling unexpected events. And they must be quick-thinking, compassionate, and levelheaded.

TRAINING

No matter what position you are hired for, you will need training. Inevitably, the training you will receive depends on the position you will be filling. Some support positions may need only minimal guidance. Other jobs may require many weeks of specialized study.

For example, if you are hired as an HSI special agent, ERO deportation officer, or ERO immigration enforcement agent, you will receive about twenty-two weeks of basic training at the ICE Academy. This facility is located on the grounds of the 1,600-acre Federal Law Enforcement Training Center in Glynco, Georgia.

Basic training at Glynco covers a wide range of topics, from communication skills to general knowledge of the law (especially immigration law), downed-officer rescues, and enforcement techniques and procedures. Firearms training is another important aspect, since agents will on occasion find it necessary to carry or use a variety of handguns and shoulder firearms.

During training, you will also become familiar with a variety of methods the agency uses to detect smuggling. You will further learn how to handle cargo searches, how to process seizures, how to deal with border violence, and how to investigate assaults on officers and U.S. citizens if the incidents are part of ICE-related cases. You also will be trained in intervention procedures, such as those used for boarding vessels and dealing with the crews of ships in port.

Furthermore, you will have extensive education in many aspects of human smuggling. Among these are the characteristics of victims of human trafficking or **indentured servitude**; falsified documents; and evidence of identity fraud or marriage fraud, which is marriage that has been arranged illegally to bring a noncitizen into the country under false pretenses.

Even after graduation, depending on your job, you may be required to take additional specialized training. You will also be expected to attend refresher courses and to participate in additional training (such as in new types of technology) throughout your career. This is true not just for special agents but for many other professional employees and support staff, as well.

SALARY AND BENEFITS

One of the most important benefits that come with a job in ICE, as in other branches of Homeland Security, is the knowledge that you are doing some good in the world. You will be helping in the defense of your nation, apprehending criminals, and protecting victims of human trafficking, or supporting these important activities.

In addition to awareness of a worthy career, ICE offers its employees a range of compensation packages that include salaries and benefits. The specifics of these differ according to the position.

Since ICE employees (like all DHS employees) work for the federal government, their salaries are determined by the same guidelines that affect all federal employees. As of early 2011, for example, an ICE investigative assistant had a base salary of about $31,300. New special agents made between $35,000 and $41,500, depending on prior experience. Highly trained IT specialists, meanwhile, received significantly more money: a base salary of about $74,000.

In addition to their salaries, ICE employees receive the standard benefits that all full-time federal workers receive.

These include health care plans, life insurance, retirement plans, and savings plans designed to help you put aside your money wisely.

Employees are also eligible for paid vacation days, sick leave, and other days off. These days off depend on seniority: the longer you have worked at the agency, the more you will accumulate. ICE agents are also given other, smaller benefits, such as being able to take their government-owned vehicles home. If uniforms are required, the agency provides an annual allowance for buying and maintaining the clothes.

FOUR

THE

COAST GUARD

THE COAST GUARD DOESN'T FIT EASILY INTO A BOX. In times of armed conflict, it can be a branch of the armed services; in peacetime, it's part of Homeland Security. Nor does the Coast Guard have its headquarters in the Pentagon, as do all other branches of the military. Although much of what the Coast Guard does takes place on or in water, a great deal happens on shore, too.

On top of that, guardians—as members of the Coast Guard are called—have been involved in every major conflict since the Civil War, but their most important work happens in peacetime. Unlike other military forces, guardians are law enforcement agents who on a given day might arrest as many people as they protect.

In short, the Coast Guard is not simply one thing or the other. It's a unique organization with a wide range of duties and powers—and so it's an especially challenging, rewarding place of work.

This U.S. Navy Coast Guard ship is cruising the waters to protect U.S. citizens.

Although the Coast Guard has been part of the Department of Homeland Security since the period after 9/11, it was created in 1790, shortly after America won independence from England. Its purpose then was twofold: to collect taxes from seagoing merchants and smugglers (who were often tolerated), as well as to catch pirates who plied the waters off the U.S. coastline.

This gives the Coast Guard far and away the longest history of any branch of Homeland Security. In fact, it is the oldest continuously operating seagoing service in the United States. Coasties—as guardians sometimes call themselves—like to point out that their predecessors dealt with homeland security for more than two centuries before the Department of Homeland Security even existed.

WHAT THE COAST GUARD DOES

The Coast Guard's mission statement lists its three basic duties: safety, security, and **stewardship**. Using these as its guidelines, the agency has developed a strong reputation for responding quickly and efficiently to emergencies and fast-changing situations. The organization's motto reflects this attitude: *Semper Paratus*—always ready.

Broadly speaking, guardians are responsible for overseeing some 361 U.S. ports and about 95,000 miles (150,000 km) of waterways, both on the sea and in major inland waterways such as the Great Lakes. This overall mission means that the Coast Guard works closely with ICE and other agencies to monitor and protect the nation's seaports, refineries, coastlines, and shipyards.

The Coast Guard's primary role today, the one it is best known for, is search and rescue. This part of the organization's work encompasses a broad range of situations. For example, Coast Guard helicopters routinely bring injured or ill fishers back to land from ships that are far offshore. Its airborne teams search for missing light aircraft or boats in U.S. waters, rescuing those aboard if possible. Sometimes the Coast Guard takes part in more unusual operations, such as coming to the aid of snowmobilers who have fallen through ice on one of the Great Lakes.

Although rescue operations are the core of the Coast Guard's tasks, it has many other responsibilities as well. One of these is enforcing laws to stop smuggling operations. The organization routinely stops and searches suspicious vessels and, if appropriate, issues subpoenas and makes arrests.

THE COAST GUARD AND KATRINA

When Hurricane Katrina devastated New Orleans and the region around it in 2005, the Coast Guard garnered high marks for the speed, effectiveness, and efficiency of its rescue efforts. Guardians rescued or evacuated more than 33,500 people, six times as many as it had saved in all of 2004. Furthermore, the Coast Guard was saving lives before any other federal agency even started despite the fact that nearly half of its locally stationed personnel had just lost their own homes.

One of the Coast Guard's many success stories involved Anna Steel, a reservist from St. Louis, Missouri, who was twenty-four years old when Katrina hit. Three days after the storm, Steel and another guardian steered a 16-foot skiff through the flooded streets of the ruined city's neighborhoods. They located thirty-five people and brought them to safety, finding dry land and temporary shelter for them on a highway on-ramp.

Despite her relatively young age, Steel led this and other rescue operations. This was because she already had extensive experience in piloting the boat—and was ready to take command. She commented later to a reporter, "[Whenever] we're out on the boat, I'm in charge. Even if my crewman is a lieutenant, which way outranks me, he reports to me. I had that authority within my first two years in the Coast Guard."

Above: U.S. Coast Guard swimmer Jerry Hoover hoists a man to safety after he was rescued from the top of a vehicle in the flooded streets of New Orleans during Hurricane Katrina.

(The Coast Guard's ability to arrest suspected criminals is unique among the U.S. military branches.)

The Coast Guard also takes on a number of other, more peaceful **maritime** tasks. For example, it maintains and manages navigational aids for maritime traffic. These include such beacons for safe passage as lighthouses, buoys, and offshore ships equipped as mobile lighthouses. Coast Guard personnel are also responsible for reporting environmental crises such as oil spills and assisting to control the damage.

When carrying out these various duties, the Coast Guard works closely with other government and military groups. These include the U.S. Navy, the Marine Corps, the federal Drug Enforcement Agency (DEA), the Bureau of Immigration and Customs Enforcement (ICE), and the federal Environmental Protection Agency (EPA).

VESSELS AND OTHER EQUIPMENT

Performing these jobs requires a broad range of tools and technology. A key element in this regard, of course, is a wide variety of boats, ships, and other waterborne vessels.

The Coast Guard classifies any vessel under 65 feet (20 meters) in length as a boat. The smallest motorized boats in the agency's fleet are 12 feet (3.5 m) long. Some of its vessels, such as inflatable rafts, are even smaller. The Coast Guard's roughly 1,400 small boats are typically used for search-and-rescue missions, port security, and the maintenance of navigational aids.

Meanwhile, ships that are 65 feet (20 m) or over are called cutters. (The name is an old word for a type of sailboat.) Typically, the Coast Guard's approximately 250 cutters are used for such duties as intercepting vessels believed to be engaging in criminal activities, breaking up ice floes (typically to clear ice-clogged shipping lanes), handling port security, making routine patrols, and maintaining seagoing navigational aids.

The Coast Guard does not just work on the water. It also has a fleet of aircraft. As of early 2011, guardians operated more than two hundred fixed-wing airplanes (turboprops and jets), as well as rotary-wing aircraft (helicopters). In addition, the Coast Guard is developing a fleet of vertical unmanned aerial vehicles (VUAVs).

Also aiding the Coast Guard in its duties is an extensive network of communications and navigational equipment. This system includes a series of full-time radio stations, as well as communications devices aboard its vessels and aircraft.

Legally, Coast Guard personnel can carry service-issued handguns on and off base, and they are issued pistols. However, the weapons are rarely carried, since many commanding officers prefer their crews to store all firearms when their use isn't anticipated. In some cases, such as drug interdiction missions, Coast Guard personnel can also be equipped with shotguns, rifles, and machine guns.

ENLISTED PERSONNEL AND OFFICERS

Maintaining and using so much equipment, as well as performing the Coast Guard's many other duties, is clearly a huge task. It takes a lot of people to keep everything running smoothly. In early 2011, about 38,000 guardians were on active duty, plus about 8,000 in its reserve forces. In addition, the Coast Guard has about 7,500 full-time civilian employees and roughly 35,000 volunteers in its auxiliary (volunteer force).

Since search-and-rescue operations are such a big part of the Coast Guard's job, it needs specialists who have a broad range of skills, from pilots and divers to mechanics and communications coordinators. The position of rescue swimmer was demonstrated in the Kevin Costner–Ashton Kutcher movie, *The Guardian*. Especially in life-threatening situations that arise in sparsely populated regions, rescue swimmers and their colleagues can be the first responders to emergencies—or the only responders. In a 2005 *Time* magazine interview, rescue swimmer Wil Milam commented about his home base in Alaska, "We're pretty much the area ambulance service."

Guardians perform many other tasks beyond search and rescue, and so the service offers a broad range of work possibilities. Most of the positions in the Coast Guard's active force are filled by enlisted personnel. Key positions to which you might be assigned as an enlisted person include small-boat operator, maintenance specialist, electronics technician, communications specialist, ship's cook, or mechanic. If you play an instrument, you might be chosen to perform in the Coast Guard's official band.

In short, enlisted personnel are the nuts and bolts that keep things running day to day. You could even say that they keep the Coast Guard afloat. As the service's website points out, "Without these individuals, the Coast Guard's daily operations would grind to a halt."

The next step up in rank from enlisted personnel is the classification of noncommissioned officer (NCO). As the name indicates, NCOs are officers who have management responsibilities but have not received **commissions**. In the Coast Guard, noncommissioned officers are called petty officers.

Higher up the chain of command are commissioned officers, who are charged with supervising NCOs. Commissioned officers are typically promoted over time to higher ranks. The primary ranks of commissioned officers rise from ensign through lieutenant, commander, and captain to admiral.

RESERVISTS, CIVILIANS, AND AUXILIARISTS

Not all guardians are full-time personnel on active duty. Like other military organizations, the Coast Guard maintains a reserve force of personnel who can be called into active duty as needed in case of natural disasters, terrorist attacks, or other emergencies.

Being a reservist is an excellent option if you are interested in serving in the Coast Guard but want to hold down a civilian day job at the same time. Reservists drill two days a month and serve about two weeks of active duty per year. These periods are typically spent in training or in working directly alongside active-duty personnel.

More than eight thousand Coast Guard reservists fill some two hundred different job categories, particularly in maritime safety, security, and the protection of natural resources. Some are special agents for the Coast Guard Investigative Service, which investigates criminal cases inside (and occasionally outside) the organization. However, reservists do not take part in any of the Coast Guard's direct combat or law enforcement operations.

In addition to reservists, there are roughly 7,700 full-time civilian employees in the Coast Guard. As a civilian, you might fill one of a number of support positions, such as those in information technology, administration, public communications, photography—even working as a barber or post office manager serving the hundreds of personnel typically stationed on a Coast Guard base.

Another important support team is the Coast Guard Auxiliary. Auxiliarists, as they're called, are volunteers. Like reservists, auxiliarists do not take part in law enforcement or combat operations. However, as part of this group you would be responsible for many duties, notably in the public-safety aspects of the Coast Guard's work. For example, you might make vessel safety checks on civilian craft, teach classes to members of marine-related industries, or connect with the public at boat shows, regattas, maritime fireworks displays, and other public events.

WHAT'S REQUIRED

As with all agencies within DHS—indeed, all government agencies—there are certain minimum requirements. To enlist as a guardian, you must be a U.S. citizen (native or naturalized) or a resident alien. To be eligible for officer status, you must be a U.S. native or naturalized citizen.

You also need to be at least eighteen years old (or seventeen with parental consent). You must have a high school diploma, although in some cases a GED equivalent is acceptable; you cannot have more than two **dependents**; and you'll have to be ready to pass the usual checks: your financial credit, your criminal record, if any, and a background check to make sure you are eligible for security clearance.

Your qualifications are also assessed by means of basic mental, medical, and physical tests. The minimum tests for physical fitness for enlisted personnel under thirty years of age include being able to do twenty-nine pushups (for men) and twenty-three (for women); thirty-eight sit-ups in one minute (for men) and thirty-two (for women); and a 1.5-mile (2.4-km) run within 12:51 minutes for men, 15:26 for women.

If you meet these basic requirements, you are ready to fill out an online application. The next step is to talk to a nearby Coast Guard recruiter, who will give you details about what's involved and help you decide whether joining would be right for you.

BOOT CAMP FOR ENLISTED PERSONNEL

If you choose to become one of the thousands who annually join the ranks of the Coast Guard's enlisted personnel, you'll start by undergoing eight weeks of boot camp at Training Center Cape May in Cape May, New Jersey. In many ways, the experience there will be similar to what you would have in other branches of the military: tough, demanding, and rewarding.

First come a few days of intake procedures, such as receiving your uniform and other basics—as well as a haircut if necessary. After that you'll have eight weeks of being taught or drilled on such topics as teamwork, physical fitness and nutrition, marching, swimming, self-discipline, military bearing, shipboard tasks, and emergency response.

Just as crucially, you'll learn about the fundamental emotional and mental aspects of Coast Guard life. Specifically, you'll come to understand and appreciate the core values required of a guardian: honor, respect, and devotion to duty.

Those who successfully pass through boot camp training are ready for graduation. Typically, new recruits are sent to their first unit and await orders to attend advanced training at facilities called Class A schools. Recruits who have performed exceptionally well in boot camp go directly to these schools without having to wait.

BECOMING AN OFFICER

If you already know that you are interested in a career as an officer, you can apply to the U.S. Coast Guard Academy in New London, Connecticut. The academy is one of the smallest federal service academies in the United States—a four-year institution with university-level academic standards.

The minimum requirements for becoming a cadet, as academy students are called, are slightly different from those of an enlisted man or woman. You can apply to the academy if you are a U.S. citizen between the ages of seventeen and twenty-two; a high school graduate or GED recipient (or will be prior to entry); unmarried with no dependents, significant financial debt, or criminal record; and judged to have sound moral character.

The application process for entering the Coast Guard Academy is stringent. It includes submitting a personal essay as well as various academic records, such as your high school transcripts, SAT Reasoning or ACT with Writing Test scores, and written evaluations by your physical education, math, and English teachers. You will also undergo physical, medical, and mental health tests and background checks that are, if anything, even more thorough than those for enlisted personnel.

During the application process, personal interviews—alone or with family members present—are not required. However, many applicants find that these interviews are useful for reaching an understanding of what to expect. Of course, the reverse is also true: one-on-one interviews help academy administrators get to know you on a personal basis.

As is true with respect to potential enlisted personnel, reservists, and auxiliarists, minority and female applicants are actively encouraged in the academy's recruiting process. The organization's website states:

> The Academy prides itself in maintaining, developing, and promoting a community of inclusion that embodies a representative cross section of the United States. It is our belief that gender, racial, ethnic, and religious diversity is critical to the professional and personal development of future Coast Guard officers as well as the entire Academy community.

AT THE ACADEMY

You can try out life at the academy by taking part in the Coast Guard's AIM (Academy Introduction Mission) program. This weeklong "summer camp" is available to students during the summer after their junior year of high school. It will give you a chance to meet the academy's faculty and staff, learn about its programs, talk with cadets and Coast Guard professionals, and much more.

If you are accepted as a cadet, you and your classmates (typically about 250–300 drawn from a pool of 4,000 applicants) will start with seven weeks of basic training, a period known as Swab Summer. ("Swabbie" is a traditional nickname for Coast Guard and Navy personnel.)

This summer-long training camp will include rigorous classroom study and equally tough physical fitness exercises.

THE COAST GUARD ACADEMY BY THE NUMBERS

Some statistics about the U.S. Coast Guard Academy, as of 2011:

80% of graduates go to graduate school (most paid for by the Coast Guard)

85% of graduates choose to serve beyond their commitment

1,046 cadets enrolled

Forty-eight states and eleven foreign nations represented

Twenty-three varsity athletic teams

31% of cadets are women

22% of cadets are minorities

One faculty member for every eight students

Average class size is nineteen

For the class of 2015:

2,344 completed the application process

374 appointments were offered

291 of those were sworn in as cadets

52% were in the top 10% of their high school classes

85% were in the top 25% of their high school classes

84% earned a varsity letter in high school

60% were team captains in high school

45% have a parent who has served in the military

BENEFITS AND OBLIGATIONS FOR
ENLISTED PERSONNEL

No matter where you stand within the Coast Guard's ranks of officers and enlisted personnel, the organization will have certain expectations of you. Notably, you must promise to serve for at least eight years. Typically, this translates to four years of active duty and four as a reservist.

Consider the benefits.

The Coast Guard's benefits package is one of the best around for someone just starting a career. To begin, there's the pay. As of early 2011, full-time enlisted personnel started with a $15,000 annual salary. This may seem like very little, but remember that the cost of meals, lodging, and many incidentals are part of the deal. Plus, after the first year, you'll be eligible for escalating pay raises, depending on your rank and how long you have been in service. These raises follow the same guidelines used in all other branches of the U.S. military.

The Coast Guard also covers costs connected to training for your specific job. In addition, it will help you pay for further education at a college or vocational school. Then there are the important considerations of free medical, dental, and eye insurance, to cover medical expenses; life and accident insurance, to help your family if you are injured or killed while on duty; and thirty days of paid vacation a year. Moreover, shopping privileges at stores on military bases, which are typically cheaper than regular stores, as well as access to gyms and other recreational facilities, are also included.

There are other excellent benefits, too. Enlisted personnel with families, for example, can choose to enroll in a health insurance plan that will cover the entire family. Plus, both men and women can take up to two years off (without pay) to stay home with a newborn. At the end of that time, these parents may rejoin the Coast Guard at the same rank.

Then, of course, there's travel. You may get an opportunity to experience new places and new cultures while on the job. Furthermore, you can use the military's guidelines regarding space-available flights. That is, you are allowed to travel free if there is an unused seat on a Department of Defense airplane headed for your destination.

The Coast Guard will also take care of you when you're older. It offers a variety of retirement plans, including one that lets you retire with a pension after serving twenty years. This means you could retire in your early forties.

BENEFITS AND OBLIGATIONS FOR ACADEMY CADETS AND GRADUATES

Cadets attending the Coast Guard Academy enjoy some additional benefits. All tuition and room-and-board costs at the academy are covered. They even get paid to go to school. A cadet's salary while attending the academy, as of early 2011, was $11,150 annually. (Generally speaking, the bulk of this is kept by the Coast Guard to pay for uniforms, equipment, and other official expenses related to training. Each month, cadets also get a portion of their salaries for personal expenses. When you graduate, you will receive any money left over in your account.)

After graduation, your salary will follow the same guidelines as equivalent military pay grades. Starting annual pay for new graduates, as of early 2011, was well over $50,000 when housing allowances, health benefits, commissary shopping privileges, and other factors were taken into consideration. Typically, there is a pay raise every two years. Benefits such as health and life insurance, housing, meals, and retirement plans are also generous.

Furthermore, officers are eligible for all-expenses-paid advanced education. During this period, typically one to two years, you can attend school full time while continuing to receive full pay and benefits.

AN AVERAGE DAY IN THE COAST GUARD

Based on 2006 statistics, on an average day the U.S. Coast Guard will

Assist 117 people in distress

Board 122 large vessels for port safety checks

Board 196 vessels of law enforcement interest

Conduct 317 vessel safety checks and teach 63 boating safety courses

Conduct 19 commercial fishing vessel safety exams

Conduct 90 search-and-rescue missions

Enforce 129 security zones

Interdict and rescue 15 illegal migrants at sea

Investigate 20 vessel casualties involving collisions and groundings

Monitor the transit of 2,557 commercial ships through U.S. ports

Process 280 mariner licenses and documents

Protect $2.8 million in property

Respond to 11 oil or hazardous chemical spills

Save 15 lives

Seize 71 pounds [32 kilograms (kg)] of marijuana and 662 pounds (300 kg) of cocaine with a street value of $21.1 million

Service 140 aids to navigation

Being selected for an advanced education program depends on your performance and potential as a student, but the chances are good that you will be accepted. For example, between 2000 and 2010, every academy graduate in engineering who applied for an engineering postgraduate program has gone on to complete a master's degree.

As is true for enlisted personnel, officers must promise to serve at least eight years, typically four on active duty and four as a reservist. If you take postgraduate training, such as flight school, you'll be required to serve a longer term, typically a minimum of five to eight years beyond the minimum.

Reservists, meanwhile, get the same pay (adjusted on an hourly or daily basis) as full-time guardians of equivalent rank. Reservists also enjoy a range of other benefits. For example, they can get help with college tuition and access to low-cost health insurance plans. As with the other categories, reservists make a commitment to serve a minimum of eight years.

AFTER YOUR COAST GUARD CAREER

Even after you have finished your years with the Coast Guard, there will be benefits. Whether you're in the reserves or in the ranks of enlisted personnel and officers, you'll have an advantage in civilian life. This is because you'll have a highly prized set of skills. The Coast Guard website states, "Almost everything we teach carries over to the civilian workforce. In fact, companies prefer to hire Coast Guard people due to their combination of experience, discipline and readiness to assume responsibility."

FEMA

LARGE-SCALE DISASTERS, BOTH NATURAL AND human-made, happen all the time—sometimes with no warning. They kill thousands of people, create widespread misery, and cause billions of dollars in damage. In the United States, the first national responder to such crises is the Federal Emergency Management Agency (FEMA). As the FEMA website states:

> Disaster. It strikes anytime, anywhere. It takes many forms—a hurricane, an earthquake, a tornado, a flood, a fire or a hazardous spill, an act of nature or an act of terrorism. It builds over days or weeks, or hits suddenly, without warning. Every year, millions of Americans face disaster, and its terrifying consequences.

> Coming to the aid of people affected by deadly crises is FEMA's job. Its mission is to make sure that the nation can

This FEMA search-and-rescue task force conducted massive searches in Indiana neighborhoods affected by Hurricane Ike in 2008.

work together to build, sustain, and improve its ability to prepare for, minimize, and recover from any disasters that might come its way. It is high-pressure and exhausting work, with long hours and often difficult conditions, but—like jobs elsewhere in DHS—it is also challenging and rewarding.

ALL ACROSS THE COUNTRY

Helping people in the wake of catastrophe is nothing new, and FEMA has existed in its present form since 1979. Like other disaster-related agencies that existed before 9/11, it became part of Homeland Security when the government's security operations were consolidated under DHS.

Today FEMA has more than 3,700 full-time employees. Some work at the agency's headquarters in Washington, D.C. Other FEMA personnel work out of regional offices across the country. Still others are stationed at the agency's operational headquarters. These are located at the Mount Weather Emergency Operations Center, the MWEOC, in the Blue Ridge Mountains west of D.C. This facility is a large and heavily secured area both above- and belowground.

In addition to its full-time professionals, FEMA employs roughly 4,000 part-time or temporary workers. When a disaster strikes, these men and women stand ready to respond at a moment's notice, eager to go wherever they are needed.

FEMA and its employees don't handle crises alone, of course. The agency works closely with other organizations to make sure that the nation's emergency management system is fully operational. Among these partners are local, state, and regional disaster relief agencies, as well as twenty-seven other federal agencies and NGOs such as the American Red Cross.

FEMA, with its huge resources, is typically the primary organization in the face of major emergencies and disasters—catastrophes that are too devastating for smaller local agencies to handle without assistance. Before FEMA can act, however, local government authorities typically must submit a formal request. Generally, this involves an affected state's governor officially declaring a state of emergency and asking the federal government for help, both financially and through direct participation.

However, there are exceptions to this broad rule. Under certain circumstances, FEMA does not need a formal request from a state. For example, if an emergency involves federal land or property, FEMA has the authority to act on its own. One example of this was the deadly bombing of the Alfred P. Murrah

A RESCUE SCENARIO

Every search-and-rescue assignment that FEMA tackles has unique characteristics and challenges. However, there are general ways in which rescue operations proceed. The following is a typical earthquake scenario.

Local fire departments and emergency management personnel, and members of local and state law enforcement agencies, are the first responders. If the local emergency manager thinks additional assistance is warranted, he or she can request it from the state. If necessary, the governor will request federal assistance.

FEMA deploys three of its closest task forces. On arrival, specialists in structural engineering determine the safety of buildings and the risk of their collapsing again.

The most massive rubble and debris is removed by heavy equipment.

A search team examines collapsed buildings and nearby areas, stabilizing and shoring up structures to make them stronger while searching for trapped people. They use equipment and aids such as electronic listening devices, small search video cameras, and search dogs.

When a victim is located, the search group begins the rescue, if necessary breaking and cutting through thousands of pounds of concrete, metal, and wood.

Teams of trauma physicians, emergency room nurses, and paramedics provide medical care for victims and rescuers. They work out of a fully stocked mobile emergency room. Medics may need to enter a collapsed structure to provide immediate aid.

Hazardous materials specialists evaluate the site; they also test persons who were exposed to hazardous chemicals, decaying bodies, or similar health risks and decontaminate those who need this treatment.

Rescue efforts continue with some 16,000 pieces of equipment. These range from heavy machinery, such as cranes and bulldozers, to smaller items such as concrete cutting saws, tents, cots, food, and water.

Information and communication specialists make sure that all team members can communicate with one another.

Once the immediate danger is over and survivors have been rescued, cleanup operations begin.

Federal Building in Oklahoma City, Oklahoma, in 1995. Similarly, when the space shuttle *Columbia* blew up in 2003, FEMA went into action without waiting to be asked.

FEET ON THE GROUND

FEMA focuses a significant amount of its resources on preparedness—that is, maintaining supplies and conducting public classes as precautions against possible crises. The clear intent is to stop the crisis before it happens, or at least to minimize the damage when it does. Dave Gilmore, a security consultant, comments, "You're trying to find out the types of problems you're dealing with and how to solve these problems in advance. Typically, you have plans to deal with the more likely problems, but you can't prepare for every eventuality. You also need to be able to react."

For example, the agency works together with other organizations to create programs that make it easier for people and businesses around the country to volunteer their time, money, and services in times of crisis. FEMA also offers training courses that are available to local relief agencies, so that they can be ready when a disaster strikes.

Some of these training courses are held locally and some are available online. Still others take place at centralized FEMA facilities such as the National Emergency Training Center in Emmitsburg, Maryland.

However, the bulk of FEMA's work takes place during or just after a crisis, providing extensive "feet on the ground" assistance. FEMA services include sending experts in specific fields to provide their knowledge, deliver specialized equipment, and establish systems to provide food and shelter to survivors.

To handle these complex jobs, FEMA is organized into a number of specialized groups, both small and large, to handle various aspects and kinds of emergencies. For example, FEMA's Mobile Emergency Response Support (MERS) teams coordinate a number of aspects of crisis management. One MERS task is to quickly establish communications with the outside world. To do this, the teams bring to the site and operate specialized equipment such as trucks with satellite uplinks, computers, portable cell phone towers, and power generators.

USAR

Other FEMA teams are responsible for other aspects of emergency work. The agency's Urban Search and Rescue (USAR) task forces provide one example. The USAR's particular focus, as the name indicates, is on operations in cities and other urban areas. It specializes in finding and retrieving victims of earthquakes, hurricanes, and other disasters. The USAR task forces often concentrate on search-and-rescue operations that involve forms of structural collapse—that is, buildings, overhead highways, and the like.

Typically, USAR task forces are made up of two teams, each with thirty-one people and four search-and-rescue dogs, plus all needed equipment. As a member of a USAR team, you might be a specialist in an area such as hazardous materials (HAZMAT) protection, emergency medicine, the decontamination of people exposed to chemical and biological agents, prescription drug dispensation, veterinary care, or the operation of heavy machinery designed to clear rubble. USAR's task forces are on constant alert, with their members working in shifts to provide twenty-four-hour readiness, seven days a week.

Standard procedure for USAR is to send the three closest task forces—that is, six teams—to an affected region within six hours of notification. If needed, more USAR teams will be flown in. As they search for and recover as many victims as possible, the USAR task forces supply emergency medical aid to the injured until transfer to a hospital can be arranged.

In addition to operating USAR task forces and other teams within the agency during a crisis, FEMA routinely coordinates its efforts with a number of groups from other federal agencies. For example, it works closely with the National Disaster Medical System (NDMS), which is part of the U.S. Department of Health and Human Services. NDMS focuses on long-range, wide-scale planning and coordination of emergency services. Of course, FEMA also works with any appropriate local agencies as well.

In addition to maintaining preparedness and providing emergency help during and immediately after catastrophes, FEMA plays a major role in what happens in the aftermath of a disaster, as areas struggle to recover from the crisis. For example, it coordinates rebuilding efforts in destroyed or damaged regions of the country. The agency also provides loans to local governments and individuals so that affected regions can recover as quickly as possible. And it works with relief NGOs, such as the Red Cross and the National Emergency Response Team, on such tasks as coordinating rescue operations and administering donations of money and supplies.

Hurricane Katrina destroyed the Tiboli Hotel and Grand Casino in Biloxi, Mississippi. FEMA brought in firefighters and other rescue workers to look for victims.

TYPES OF JOBS

Clearly, considering the broad scope and different kinds of emergency work the agency handles, FEMA needs to find people who are skilled in many different aspects of disaster prevention and relief. Because of this, a wide variety of positions are available for those considering a career with this important organization.

Broadly speaking, FEMA's occupations are divided into a number of specialized groups. The agency calls these groups cadres. Some cadres operate nationally, while some are responsible for specific regions.

Within cadres, there are even more specialized positions. Among these are jobs that focus on areas such as telecommunications, information technology, logistical planning, security, training, forensic science, hazardous waste containment and disposal, and medicine. Furthermore, FEMA is always in need of employees who are able to work on road crews and as emergency-call personnel, as well as people who are skilled in carpentry, architecture, vehicle maintenance and driving, and heavy equipment operation.

Even more unusual positions, such as those filled by archaeologists and environmental or historical preservation specialists, are among the jobs available in FEMA's cadres. As much as possible in a post-disaster period, these employees work to preserve a region's cultural and natural treasures, which may include important buildings, natural formations like coastlines and wilderness areas, or Native American burial grounds.

Each cadre has a core group of permanent, full-time employees. However, each also includes a number of temporary employees who fill vacancies or work on specific, short-term projects. In addition, FEMA has many disaster assistance employees (DAEs). The men and women of the DAE teams are considered to be reservists. They are typically hired for a two-year period (which can be extended) and work on an on-call, intermittent basis—meaning they have day jobs but are prepared to go into action for FEMA when disaster strikes.

SCEP AND STEP

If you are interested in one of the positions FEMA offers, you will have an opportunity to learn about it when you are in high school or college. Like other branches of Homeland Security, FEMA offers a number of ways for students to take part in internships, summer job positions, and volunteer programs.

The main branch of FEMA that is devoted to bringing in interns is called the Student Educational Employment Program (SEEP). SEEP has two components: the Student Career Experience Program (SCEP) and the Student Temporary Employment Program (STEP). Together, these programs accept students who are in high school, vocational and technical school, two- or four-year colleges, or graduate or professional degree school.

If you become part of SCEP, you will take part in FEMA activities while attending school. SCEP is designed for students who want FEMA work experience that is directly related to their field of study. In this way, participation in the program results in a direct extension of your major academic interests. For example, if you are a finance major, you would work in one of the FEMA divisions that focuses on the agency's finance and budgetary needs.

Meanwhile, STEP is for students who want FEMA work experience even if it is not directly related to academic or career goals. Unlike participants in SCEP, STEP students do not have work schedules that are tied to the academic year. They can (and often do) work at FEMA full time or part time at any point throughout the year.

There are no limitations on the number of hours a student can work per week, for either SCEP or STEP. However, your work schedule will not interfere with your academic schedule.

Another difference between SCEP and STEP concerns what happens when your period of work is over. After graduation from SCEP you will have the opportunity to be hired for a permanent position. This conversion (as the transition from student to full-time employee is called) requires a minimum of

Internships in ICPD, as with other divisions of FEMA's student programs, can be full time or part time, and the job's hours are flexible to fit the needs of its participants. Intern positions are unpaid; however, depending on your school's policies, the program may count toward college credit. Furthermore, some interns will have the option of automatic conversion to career appointments.

There is yet another way for students to participate in FEMA; namely, by taking part in the agency's volunteer program for students. The Student Volunteer Employment Program (SVEP) recruits students to volunteer by explaining that this is a way to get valuable work experience directly related to their academic field of study. As with the FCIP program, participating students may be eligible to receive educational credit.

REQUIREMENTS

As with all departments within the DHS, the first step for applying for a job or internship with FEMA is to visit usajobs.gov. There you can use the Job Finder system to view available positions, register to create an online application, and get contact information for finding out more details. If you are applying for an internship, please be sure to do this by your junior year in college. The extensive background check takes so long that seniors are automatically ineligible.

Naturally, application requirements and deadlines will differ for each paid position, internship, or volunteer program. However, there are certain basic requirements for any candidate. First of all, as is true with other DHS jobs, you must be a U.S. citizen and pass a background check. You must also be enrolled at least half-time in an academic or vocational-technical program at an accredited educational institution. And you must be at least sixteen years old.

Qualifications for many positions of regular employment with FEMA include, as a minimum, having a bachelor's degree from an accredited four-year college, as well as passing a test called the Administrative Career with America (ACWA) test. These requirements apply to all federal employees who enter the system at a level above the lowest.

To become an intern in FEMA's other programs, additional qualifications may be needed. For example, the requirements for members of the Individual and Community Preparedness Division (ICPD) are extensive. You will be expected to have excellent computer skills, including experience with Internet research and proficiency with the Microsoft Office Suite (Word, PowerPoint, Excel, Outlook).

When applying for a student position, you will also need to submit certain forms, which include a resumé outlining your education, work, and other experiences. (The same is true for student and other positions elsewhere in Homeland Security.) Furthermore, you will need to provide copies of your school transcripts, as well as three personal references from people who are not family members.

Requirements for regular employment with FEMA vary depending on the specific department and position. DAEs and reservists, for example, must be able to leave their regular jobs quickly, often with less than a day's notice, and be prepared to stay away for long periods, often a month or more. They must also be prepared to work long hours and, if necessary, every day of the week. And they must be willing to work irregular hours. So people who take a DAE or reservist position typically cannot rely on the job as their only means of support. As the FEMA website states, "[They] must consider the Reservist Program as an intermittent source of income."

Furthermore, DAEs, reservists, and all other employees within FEMA need to be highly motivated, with the ability to think quickly and work on their own with a minimum of supervision. The ability to remain cool and rational under tense situations is essential.

It is also vital—especially in the case of DAEs and others in the field—to have a high degree of sympathy and a strong desire to help others. After all, you'll be dealing with people under the worst, most trying circumstances. Disaster victims may have just lost their homes or families, or they may be seriously injured. They may be facing financial ruin and years of recovery. In any case, FEMA demands respect and compassion from the people working to save these victims of crises.

SALARIES AND BENEFITS

Overall, benefits and salaries within FEMA follow guidelines that are similar to other, related government jobs. Employees are paid according to the standard GS scale. Many FEMA employees enter at a GS-3 or GS-5 level. Full-time employees with at least a year of graduate study beyond a bachelor's degree or experience in a field associated with the job can enter the agency at a higher pay scale, typically GS-7. You can learn more about current federal pay grades at www.fedjobs.com/pay/pay.html.

Since the government considers DAEs to be temporary and

intermittent workers, they are paid on an hourly basis. As of 2011 the pay scale for DAEs ranged from $11.29 to $42.03 per hour, depending on factors such as experience and the specific job description. As a DAE, you will be paid for the hours spent traveling to and from a disaster site. A per-diem (per-day) allowance is also supplied to cover food, lodging, and other expenses while on the job. If you work more than eight hours per day or forty hours per week, you will receive overtime pay.

The pay for full-time, permanent FEMA employees is competitive, overtime is compensated, and there always is potential for promotion and pay increases based on such factors as performance, seniority, and the specific job. For example, the base pay for a full-time security guard as of 2011 was about $30,700. A public affairs specialist, meanwhile, earned about $68,800.

Benefits for full-time employees, such as health insurance, sick days, vacation time, and pension plans, are similar to those for other federal employees. Temporary employees are not eligible for many of these benefits. On the other hand, they can earn sick and vacation days based on the amount of time they have spent working. Furthermore, they are covered by Social Security and unemployment compensation. They can buy health insurance through FEMA after one year of temporary service.

Of course, salaries and benefits are not the only rewards for working in DHS. No matter what part of Homeland Security you are interested in joining—TSA, ICE, USCG, FEMA, or any other of the many other agencies within Homeland Security, you will have an intangible profit: the knowledge that you are part of an organization devoted to the vital task of keeping your country safe and healthy.

GLOSSARY

biometrics—The science of using physical traits or characteristics to identify people.

commission—A formal document declaring that a member of the military has joined the upper officer class.

contraband—Illegal or smuggled items, such as guns or drugs.

cybersecurity—Work aimed at preventing crimes that are committed via the Internet (cybercrimes).

dependents—People, typically children, who must rely on someone else for income.

indentured servitude—A form of employment so harsh that it amounts to slavery.

infrastructure—The underlying structure of a city or government, such as a police force or tax system.

intelligence data—Information that can be used by specialists to determine such things as potential terror threats.

interdiction—Interception, especially for illegal activities.

INTERPOL—The world's largest international police organization.

maritime—Having to do with the sea.

NGOs—Nongovernmental organizations, such as the International Red Cross.

noninvasive—With minimal or no intrusion into a person's privacy or body.

prosthetic—Artificial; a prosthetic arm replaces one that has been lost.

resumé—Also called a C.V.; a summary of a person's academic, life, and work experiences and accomplishments.

stewardship—The responsibility for taking care of something.

tariff—A form of taxation.

NOTES

INTRODUCTION

p. 6, "I'd say . . .": Quoted in Elka Jones, "Careers in Homeland Security," *Career Outlook Quarterly*, Summer 2006, http://findarticles.com/p/articles/mi_qa5448/is_200607/ai_n21393356/.

NOTES

pp. 8–9, "The mission . . .": Department of Homeland Security, "President Establishes Office of Homeland Security," www.dhs. gov/xnews/releases/press_release_0010.shtm.

p. 9, "In 2010 . . .": Quoted in Dana Priest and William M. Arkin, "Monitoring America," *Washington Post*, December 12, 2010, http://projects.washingtonpost.com/top-secret-america/ articles/monitoring-america/1/.

pp. 9–10, "Homeland Security's . . .": Quoted in Jones, "Careers in Homeland Security".

p. 11, "In an article . . .": Quoted in Amanda Ripley, "Hurricane Katrina: How the Coast Guard Gets It Right," *Time*, October 23, 2005, www.time.com/time/magazine/article/ 0,9171,1122007-4,00.html.

CHAPTER 1

p. 15, "[E]very day, . . .": Message from the Secretary, *Quadrennial Homeland Security Review Report*, February 2010, http//www.dhs. gov/xlibrary/assets/qhsr_report.pdf.

p. 15, "Kenneth St. Germain . . .": Quoted in Elka Jones, "Careers in Homeland Security,"*Career Outlook Quarterly*, Summer 2006, http://findarticles.com/p/articles/mi_qa5448/is_200607/ ai_n21393356/.

p. 16, "One member of this group . . .": Quoted in Dana Priest and William M. Arkin, "Monitoring America," *Washington Post*, December 12, 2010, http://projects.washingtonpost.com/ top-secret-america/articles/monitoring-america/1/.

p. 17, "An article in . . .": Quoted in Nathan Olivarez-Giles, "Homeland Security to issue terror alerts on Facebook, Twitter; nix color system, " *Los Angeles Times*, April 7, 2011, http://latimesblogs.latimes.com/technology/2011/04/ homeland-security-may-issue-terror-alerts-on-facebook -twitter-axe-color-system.html.

CHAPTER 2

p. 38, "In a 2005 article . . .": Quoted in Sara Kehaulani Goo, "Marshals to Patrol Land, Sea Transport," *Washington Post*,

December 14, 2005, www.washingtonpost.com/wp-dyn/
content/article/2005/ 12/13/AR2005121301709.html.

p. 41, "Many air passengers are . . .": Blogger Bob, "Lady Gaga's
Handcuffs & The TSA Permitted/Prohibited Items List," *The
TSA Blog*, September 22, 2010, http://blog.tsa.gov/2010/09/
lady-gagas-handcuffs-tsa.html.

p. 43, "As the agency's . . .": Anonymous, "Federal Air Marshal Service Careers," TSA.gov, www.tsa.gov/lawenforcement/people/
fams_join.shtm.

p. 46, "TSA is going to . . .": Quoted in Goo, "Marshals to Patrol
Land, Sea Transport,".

p. 47, "In a *Washington Post* . . .": Quoted in Goo, "Marshals to
Patrol Land, Sea Transport."

CHAPTER 3

p. 52, "As the HSI website . . . ": Anonymous, "Are You Ready for
the Challenge?" ICE, hwww.ice.gov/doclib/xml/movie-cap-
tion/hsi_1811.xml.

CHAPTER 4

p. 73, "In a 2005 *Time* article . . . ": Quoted in Amanda Ripley,
"Hurricane Katrina: How the Coast Guard Gets It Right,"
Time, October 23, 2005, www.time.com/time/magazine/
article/0,9171,1122007-4,00.html.

p. 73, "As the service's . . . ": Anonymous, "Careers," Coast Guard,
www.uscg.mil/top/careers.asp.

p. 78, "The Academy prides itself . . . ": Anonymous, "Careers,"
Coast Guard..

p. 85, "The Coast Guard website . . . ": Anonymous, "Careers,"
Coast Guard.

CHAPTER 5

p. 86, "Disaster. It strikes anytime . . . ": Anonymous, "About
FEMA," FEMA, www.fema.gov/about/.

p. 90, "Dave Gilmore, . . . ": Quoted in Elka Jones, "Careers in
Homeland Security," *Career Outlook Quarterly*, Summer

2006, http://findarticles.com/p/articles/mi_qa5448/is_200607/ai_n21393356/.

p. 100, "As the FEMA website . . . ": Anonymous, "Terms of Employment," FEMA, www.fema.gov/about/career/terms.shtm.

p. 89, "Every search-and-rescue assignment . . . ": Source: Anonymous, "Profile of a Rescue," *www.fema.gov/emergency/usr/profile.shtm.*

FURTHER INFORMATION

BOOKS

Doak, Robin S. *Homeland Security*. New York: Children's Press, 2011.

Kleyn, Tatyana. *Immigration: The Ultimate Teen Guide*. Lanham, MD: Scarecrow Press, 2011.

Learning Express editors. *Becoming a Homeland Security Professional*. New York: Learning Express, 2011.

McDonnell, Julia. *Coast Guard*. New York: Gareth Stevens Publishing, 2011.

Thompson, Kalee. *Deadliest Sea: The Untold Story Behind the Greatest Rescue in Coast Guard History*. New York: HarperCollins, 2011.

WEBSITES

Department of Homeland Security
www.dhs.gov/index.shtm

Department of Homeland Security Blog
http://blog.dhs.gov

Federal Emergency Management Agency
www.fema.gov

FEMA Blog
http://blog.fema.gov

Immigration and Customs Enforcement
www.ice.gov

Transportation Security Administration
www.tsa.gov

TSA Blog
    http://blog.tsa.gov
U.S. Coast Guard Academy
    www.cga.edu
U.S. Coast Guard
    www.uscg.mil
U.S. Coast Guard Blog
    http://cgblog.org

BIBLIOGRAPHY

BOOKS

Carter, Stephen L. *The Violence of Peace*. New York: Beast Books, 2011.
Hutton, Donald B. and Mydlarz. *Guide to Homeland Security Careers*. Hauppauge, NY: Barron's Educational Series, 2003.
USCG. *U.S. Coast Guard: The Shield of Freedom*, USCG, Washington, DC, 2003.

PERIODICALS AND WEBSITES

Anonymous. "Are You Ready for the Challenge?" www.ice.gov/doclib/xml/movie-caption/hsi_1811.xml.
Anonymous. "President Establishes Office of Homeland Security." Department of Homeland Security. www.dhs.gov/xnews/releases/press_release_0010.shtm.
Anonymous. "Federal Air Marshal Service Careers." www.tsa.gov/lawenforcement/people/fams_join.shtm.
Anonymous. "Careers." www.uscg.mil/top/careers.asp.
Anonymous. "Careers." www.cga.edu/display.aspx?id=12847.
Anonymous. "About FEMA." www.fema.gov/about/.
Anonymous. "Terms of Employment." www.fema.gov/about/career/terms.shtm.
Goo, Sara Kehaulani. "Marshals to Patrol Land, Sea Transport." *Washington Post*, December 14, 2005. www.washingtonpost.com/wp-dyn/content/article/2005/12/13/AR2005121301709.html.

Jones, Elka. "Careers in Homeland Security." *Career Outlook Quarterly*, Summer 2006. http://findarticles.com/p/articles/mi_qa5448/is_200607/ai_n21393356/.

Napolitano, Janet. "Message from the Secretary," Department of Homeland Security. *Quadrennial Homeland Security Review Report*, February 2010. www.dhs.gov/xlibrary/assets/cfo-afrfy2010-vol1.pdf.

Olivarez-Giles, Nathan. "Homeland Security to issue terror alerts on Facebook, Twitter; nix color system." *Los Angeles Times*, April 7, 2011. http://latimesblogs.latimes.com/technology/2011/04/homeland-security-may-issue-terror-alerts-on-facebook-twitter-axe-color-system.html.

Priest, Dana, and Arkin, William M.. "Monitoring America." *Washington Post*, December 12, 2010. http://projects.washingtonpost.com/top-secret-america/articles/monitoring-america/1/.

Ripley, Amanda. "Hurricane Katrina: How the Coast Guard Gets It Right." *Time*, October 23, 2005, www.time.com/time/magazine/article/0,9171,1122007-4,00.html.

USCG. *U.S. Coast Guard: America's Maritime Guardian*, USCG (electronic resource),www.uscg.mil/history/allen/docs/USCG_Pub1_2002.pdf.

INDEX

INDEX

ABOUT THE AUTHOR

ADAM WOOG is the author of many books for adults, young adults, and children. His most recent books are *Military Might and Global Intervention* in the Controversy! series, and the five other titles in this series. Woog lives in his hometown of Seattle, Washington, with his wife. Their daughter, a college student, is majoring in criminal justice and criminology.